The Secrets of your Divine Powers

Reconnect with your Spiritual Self to Overcome Obstacles, Heal your Life, and Achieve True Success

Henry Thomas Hamblin

Hamblin Vision Publishing

Copyright

 Copyright 2024 Hamblin Vision Publishing - all rights reserved.

The content contained within this book may not be reproduced, duplicated or transmitted without direct written permission from the author or the publisher.

Under no circumstances will any blame or legal responsibility be held against the publisher, or author, for any damages, reparation, or monetary loss due to the information contained within this book, either directly or indirectly.

Legal Notice:

This book is copyright protected. It is only for personal use. You cannot amend, distribute, sell, use, quote or paraphrase any part, or the content within this book, without the consent of the author or publisher.

Disclaimer Notice:

Please note the information contained within this document is for educational and entertainment purposes only. All effort has been executed to present accurate, up to date, reliable, complete information. No warranties of any kind are declared or implied. Readers acknowledge that the author is not engaged in the rendering of legal, financial, medical or professional advice. The content within this book has been derived from various sources. Please consult a licensed professional before attempting any techniques outlined in this book.

By reading this document, the reader agrees that under no circumstances is the author responsible for any losses, direct or indirect, that are incurred as a result of the use of the information contained within this document, including, but not limited to, errors, omissions, or inaccuracies.

Introduction

BY NOEL RAINE, CHAIR OF THE HAMBLIN TRUST

Henry Thomas Hamblin was a prolific author of a range of books, booklets and pamphlets offering practical advice on how to live in harmony with God, or what he sometimes referred to as Source, the Universe, or the Cosmic. However, this was not just a spiritual quest, or an attempt to avoid the troubles and cares of everyday life – far from it, for Hamblin was a very practical mystic – but a practical guide to each one to follow to increase health, happiness, and prosperity.

Hamblin founded the **Science of Thought Institute**, offering a course of practical lessons intended to guide his many thousands of students towards a happier, healthier and more prosperous life and, although he is sadly no longer with us in person, he left a wonderful legacy of publications that he had written from 1921 up to the time of his death in 1958. Some of those are still in print and available from The Hamblin Trust on www.thehamblinvision.org.uk but many have since gone out of print.

Conscious that the Trust will not be around forever, the custodians of Hamblin's teachings, the trustees of the Hamblin Trust, have decided to produce copies of Hamblin's earlier works in digital format to leave a legacy for future generations. Whilst the style of writing may now seem a little dated, Hamblin's teachings remain valid and, although edited a little to bring them more into line with current editorial style, we are pleased to bring to you in one compilation, four of Hamblin's original booklets in "The Power Series" written in 1923.

- Power to be Well
- Power to Overcome
- Power to Succeed
- Power to Transform Life

It is our hope that this compilation will, indeed, help you to transform your life.

Many blessings for health, success and happiness.

Noel Raine

Chair of the trustees

The Hamblin Trust

Concise Biography of Henry Thomas Hamblin

By John Delafield, Hamblin's grandson

Who was Henry Thomas Hamblin?

Henry Thomas Hamblin was a spiritual teacher and writer based in Sussex, England, whose message and vision were straightforward and pragmatic. He believed that the spiritual life and the practical, everyday life were inseparable. His teachings centred around the power of thought and the importance of meditation to draw on the inner power, wisdom and love that we all have deep within us. Hamblin referred to this as "the Secret Place of the Most High" in the days before meditation was widely practiced in the West.

Hamblin was colloquially known as HTH, and later 'The Saint of Sussex'. Whilst his teachings leaned towards esoteric Christianity, his philosophy was truly universal, embracing the truths of all faiths. The emphasis of his message is on finding the power of spirituality within us all, in the context of our everyday lives, rather than religion. As a young man, he reacted against the dogma of his strict, religious upbringing, and believed that religion often divided people, while spirituality united people. His teachings came from a place of pure empathy and compassion for humankind.

Henry Thomas Hamblin worked right up to the end of his life in 1958 and left a legacy that continues to this day, its voice as much needed now as it ever was.

A Wayward Child

Henry Thomas Hamblin was born in 1873 in Walworth, South East London, of Kentish parents, and was the second of two sons. His father was very religious, and his grandfather a minister of the Baptist Church. His mother, although of diminutive size, was reportedly "great of soul" and ruled the family with benevolent autocracy. The family was poor, very poor, like all those living around them in that district of London in the late Victorian era, and, despite their hard work, the only education that could be afforded for Henry was an elementary one. He followed this with a course in technology, which proved to be of inestimable value to a youth who was considered by his parents and teachers to be wayward.

"Unstable as water; thou shall not excel," his mother reproached him regularly. No doubt she intended it to shame her son into a regime of self-improvement, in keeping with child-rearing practices of the time, but it was hardly confidence-inspiring! "Slacker!" was the repeated insult from his elder brother. Wiser, more objective, heads might have paused for long enough to recognise a certain potential in the young boy who, at the age of nine, could attempt the writing of a school newspaper. He had also established himself as something of an elocutionist. Writing and speaking would both prove valuable skills in later life.

His adolescent years gave little indication of an error in the family verdict. "Henry the wayward" moved from one poorly paid post to another, idled in between dead-end jobs, succumbed to bouts of ill-health, and, before he had reached the age of eighteen, had displayed more than the usual "adolescent failings", according to his autobiography, *The Story of My Life*. From a modern perspective, all these Victorian euphemisms point to Hamblin being something of a "bad lad", an impression added to by his own heavy hints that he had been no stranger to drinking and carousing. He suffered terribly from pangs of regret following his periods of over-indulgence, so that "Henry the sinner" became "Henry the saint" – until the next time. His pronounced rebellious streak landed him in hot water more than once. He constantly pushed against the boundaries of the fire-and-brimstone brand of Christianity in which he had been raised, which he felt to be unbearably restrictive. Reading about his struggles with authority as a young man somehow makes the rather aloof spiritual writer he became more accessible and endearing; it's hard not to warm to someone who so openly confesses their own faults and shortcomings, especially in the tightly buttoned-up era in which he lived. He was inspired by books, many of which fired his worldly ambition and prompted his spiritual imagination.

What his parents and educators overlooked was that Hamblin was a young man with huge aspiration, flushed with a youthful zest for life, and inspired by a worthy ambition to rise above the rut of his circumstances. Although he pushed against his father's dogmatic and punitive style of practising religion, at heart, he was deeply religious. A person's early environment, education, and adolescent behaviour can often determine the course of their life. Youthful indulgences of one sort or another are inevitable. Hamblin's studies of the New Testament, which revealed that selfishness and hypocrisy, rather than indulgence, received greater condemnation by Jesus, would have been very much in his consciousness.

A Successful Businessman

There is no doubt that Hamblin had an enquiring mind, and this, coupled with a desire for scientific accuracy, enabled him to achieve success in his later endeavours in business. In this, despite his lack of education, he was bolstered by boundless faith and courage, which, coupled with a shrewd business sense, ensured that he succeeded beyond all expectation. In 1898, having taught himself opthalmics at night, he qualified as an optician and set up his first successful business as an optician, Theodore Hamblin (now Dolland and Aitchison), frequented by royalty, the rich and the famous.

Hamblin was a natural entrepreneur and a born risk-taker. By this time, he was also a family man. He married Eva Elizabeth in 1902, and they went on to have two sons and a daughter.

He enjoyed acquiring several businesses, all with insufficient capital, and relying on credit and goodwill. He took more pleasure in the thrill of the challenge than in the promise of monetary gain. Far from being downcast in the face of numerous setbacks, he thrived on negotiating obstacles which appeared insurmountable. As soon as the business was established and running smoothly, however, rather than being satisfied with financial security and the ability to provide for his family, Hamblin's interest started to wane. He felt a loss of the initial drive and motivation, his physical and mental health began to decline… until the next big idea came along and away he would charge again, all fired up and raring to go.

Throughout all his wild days of youth and high-risk business ventures, Hamblin felt a great tug towards discovering a deeper meaning to life, beyond that of the daily struggle to make ends meet. Propelled by his discontent, he became a driven seeker after truth. In his quest, he met other prominent thinkers of the time and formed lasting friendships.

As his business success grew, so did a gnawing sense of depression. It was as if there was something inside him that had not yet found a voice. Around this time, he discovered the New Thought movement and began to read their publications. Hamblin realised then that none of his worldly success had made him happy. He felt that a move from London to the coast would be beneficial. Shortly afterwards came the outbreak of the First World War, and Hamblin went off to serve his country, leaving his business in the care of others, almost with a sense of gleeful relief, strange though it sounds.

But it was the sudden and unexpected death of his younger son at the age of ten, in 1918, that brought him to rock bottom and to question everything.

A Very Practical Mystic

Hamblin was not a genius, and millions of other people have made good in the world with even less promising assets. But it was in the second half of his life, when Hamblin turned away from creating highly successful business enterprises to focus instead on the spiritual realm, that his unique combination of the pragmatic and the profoundly spiritual shone forth. He has sometimes been described as a very practical mystic.

Hamblin began writing in the 1920s. The words seemed to flow from him. He found that writing clarified his thoughts. One of his first books written in this new phase of his career was *Within You Is The Power*, which was to sell over 200,000 copies. Other books soon followed. Hamblin believed that there is a source of abundance which, when contacted, could change a person's entire life. As long as people blamed their external circumstances for any misfortune, they were stuck in the 'victim role'; but if they moved in harmony with their inner source, their life could be full of abundance and harmony.

Soon after this, Hamblin set up a magazine called *The Science of Thought Review*, based on the principles of Applied Right Thinking. He wasn't discouraged by the fact that he had no experience of editing or publishing. His experience had taught him that if the mind worked in harmony with the Divine, then everything you needed flowed towards you. Anyone with any business sense at all knew that to set up a magazine with a first print run of 10,000 copies would be a risky thing to do. But Hamblin was not risk averse, to put it mildly! He wanted to put what he believed into practice. The only magazine of its kind in the 1920s, it soon gained a worldwide readership. Among his friends and contemporaries that were to contribute to the magazine were Joel Goldsmith, Henry Victor Morgan, Graham Ikin, Clare Cameron and Derek Neville, all of them prolific and successful writers. Apart from his international subscribers, Hamblin had close ties to comparative spiritual thinkers in many other countries, especially in the U.S.

Although he had been brought up in a strictly religious family, he hadn't found any of the answers he sought in the Church. He realised that, rather than following any creed or dogma, which didn't work for him anyway, he had to look within himself. He found contact with 'Presence' and realised it held the key to the peace he was seeking. All the time, his search was leading him nearer to discovering the way his thoughts affected his performance and outlook.

During the General Strike of 1926, the Great Depression of 1929-32, and again in years after the end of the Second World War, many homeless, unemployed wayfarers came to the Hamblin household seeking relief and shelter. Henry and Elizabeth provided them with a simple meal, new boots and clothing, and money for the road. Known colloquially as 'The Saint of Sussex", Hamblin was a man who applied his spiritual principles to his everyday life. Practical Mysticism was Hamblin's life's work. He helped people in deeply practical ways to become less fearful, happier, and more successful in their lives. To this end, he wrote books like *The Antidote to Worry*. However, later in life he realised that whilst these books genuinely helped people, they were largely concerned with the personality. He then wished to go a step further and become more fully a truly 'practical mystic', so he wrote a spiritual course of 26 lessons, each with a definite theme presented in a systematic way. This was designed to move beyond the constraints of personality so that the soul could breathe the pure air of Spirit. What was needed, he felt, was 'a total surrender of ourselves to the Divine.' The course is available as the book *The Way of the Practical Mystic*.

The Power of Thought

Hamblin was at the forefront of the New Thought movement which was gaining pace in the early 20th century. He discovered that 'new thought' was, in fact, ancient wisdom, based upon the truth that has always existed since before time began. All great souls give voice to that timeless truth in a myriad of different ways. Hamblin urges us to "Think in harmony with the Universal Mind." In other words, he underlines the fact that truth is and cannot be changed depending upon our mood or our whim.

Hamblin realised that we need not only a positive frame of mind but an applied way of thinking - Right Thinking, as he termed it. What did he mean by that? Well, he wrote a book on it, *The Little Book of Right Thinking*, which is in its 17th reprint. Essentially, he defines Right Thinking as:

- Thinking from the Divine standpoint.

- Controlling the thoughts so they do not go off on negative tangents away from the Divine Truth, which is always positive.

- Replacing negative thoughts with positive thoughts

- Living in the consciousness that all is well; and as an adjunct to this, remembering that perfection exists as a reality now, and to think in the consciousness of that knowledge.

- Meditation or prayer is the highest form of Right Thinking.

- Ultimately, however, the aim is to get beyond thought, 'to enter ultimate Truth'.

He says, 'When we cease thinking, we glide out on the ocean of God's Peace. Thought brings us to the foot of the mountain after which we have to proceed by intuition'.

> *'Health, Wealth and Happiness. Isn't this something we all want, either for ourselves or for those dear to us? And yet, how many of us are struggling*

to reach or hold such a goal for a sustained period of time?'

Hamblin's teachings explain how we can achieve all of these things, not by hard work and striving but by a simple change of thought. Within You is the Power is one of his simple but profound statements, and the title of one of his books.

Hamblin was a prolific author and had many thousands of followers studying and benefiting from his teachings and courses until his death in 1958. The simple principles contained in those teachings are as relevant today as they were when he was alive, and can still help us to achieve health, prosperity and happiness if we apply them conscientiously.

He died in 1958 in Chichester Hospital. The Hamblin Trust exists to this day to propagate the legacy of his work.

The Relevance of his Teachings Today

Hamblin was, essentially, a Christian mystic, yet his ideas about the simplicity and clarity of presence seem incredibly contemporary. He believed that the source of all wisdom is within us and all around us, and that this is the fundamental reality; there is no separation, and we are all one. His message and advice to all who read his work is that it is for everyone and is in harmony with the aspiration of all good people throughout time. Hamblin believed that there can be no finite creed of an infinite faith. Moreover, he suggests that, when creeds appear, true faith can be constrained.

He cautioned that if you seek God in prayer, the corollary is that you must have faith in Him. He often stressed that no prayer goes unanswered, and, although you may not get the answer requested, your prayer will be answered in some form. God is around us and within us, and this is the fundamental reality. He made it clear that, although human organisations come and go, God's laws are eternal, and that God is the quintessence of love, wisdom, and harmony. He expresses the clear view that "Blessed are they who believe and yet have not seen". The knowledge that God is born within us is fundamental to our understanding, and only by the loss of self can God be found. At the point a person surrenders his or her 'self' to God, it is then that a re-birth takes place and one's real life in God begins.

Some may question this view and ask: "What is this but the core teachings of the many brands of Christianity?" In response, Hamblin's view was that modern Christianity is a heterogeneous compound of the teachings of Jesus interwoven with historic pagan-based doubts and fears, litanies, supplications and more, all of which are closely guarded by a priestly hierarchy. These were strong views, and Hamblin does not disparage those who found them uncomfortable, as he says that churches are necessary and helpful for those who are succoured by them. Hamblin had a lifelong rebellious streak where authority was concerned, and this included the strictures of the Church. Hamblin would sometimes say that the Truth of the message of Jesus was so often wrapped up in dogma and creed that its purity and simplicity were obscured.

In his teaching, he states that first comes purity of intention, reminding his readers that one cannot serve God and Mammon. Either you trust God completely or you hedge your bets by having worldly alliances and a healthy bank balance. He maintains that trying to achieve both will impair spiritual development. Secondly, an individual's dedication to following God's path will require great patience, perseverance, faith and courage; but in following this path, the individual will develop forbearance and good will. He adds that other life experiences will follow naturally and lead to a developing compassion, which will enable the individual to radiate the love of God.

Where should we place Hamblin in the long line of mystics, seekers and finders? Perhaps it is rather impertinent to pose the question some 65 years after his death, but it is surely relevant to consider this point as, by any measure, he was an extraordinary person.

Remember that he was born into a life of poverty and obscurity but, despite a very limited education, by superhuman efforts of his imagination, he rose to wealth and secured an esteemed position in life, while all the time being aware of another "self" within him, a spiritual self. Dramatically, in the middle part of his life, he surrendered his material successes to follow his wider calling as a disciple of God. In this later life, he did not subscribe to any specific creed or form of religion. He was no haloed saint in the traditional sense, but he would have said, "What I have done, or rather what has been done through me, can be done by any person in the world according to their gifts and personal faith".

The essence of this teaching is that the latent power of God lies within everyone.

Contents

Part 1: Power to be Well
The effect of thought on health and healing

    1. The Spiritual and Mental Causes of Ill-Health   1

    2. Divine Healing   12
        Instructions for those who Wish to be Healed

    3. Thoughts and Health   20

Part 2: Power to Overcome
Overcoming Life's Difficulties

    4. Foreword   24
        by W.G. Hooper

    5. The Power is Within   29

    6. The Life of Victory   34

    7. Lions in the Path   38

    8. From Victory to Victory   41

Part 3: Power to Succeed
How to create a successful life with the power of thought

9. The Pathfinder   46
   Foreword by John R. Todd

10. What is Success?   50

11. Faith   53

12. Vision   56

13. Service   61

14. The Way of Real Success   66

Part 4: Power to Transform Life
A Thought Revolution

15. Preface   72
    by Henry Thomas Hamblin

16. Meeting Life in the Right Spirit   74

17. Life is Good   89

18. A Revolution in Our Thought Life   93

Afterword   98
Life and Power

Also by Henry Thomas Hamblin   103

Chapter One

The Spiritual and Mental Causes of Ill-Health

There is a power within us to be well. Disease, ill-health, sickness, these have no part in the divine idea. Each individual life is perfect, as it is imaged in the Divine Mind, and the extent of man's disease or sickness is the measure of his falling short of the divine or Christ ideal.

It is normal to be healthy and well, and abnormal to be sick. There is only one life, and this is divine and perfect. If this is allowed to flow freely, good health must be the natural outcome. When, however, the life stream is poisoned by hate, malice, lust, fear, worry, mistrust, and other evil thoughts, desires, passions and emotions, then sickness and disease are the natural result.

It is a well-known and established fact that hate, malice, revenge, and bad temper are highly destructive to health. They produce, in the bloodstream, poisons of a deadly character. All wrong thoughts and emotions are detrimental to health. They break down the nervous system and destroy digestion, thus making health impossible. Love is life and hate is death is eternally true and just; as hate, if indulged in, destroys health, so, in like manner, does love heal, build up and bless. Supposing a person does you an injury and you resent it, brood over it, and feel angry about it, thinking to yourself how you would like to "get your own back" and thus make him suffer in return, does it make you feel happy and fit? Does it make you sleep better, enjoy your food more and cause you to be a better friend or companion? Far from it. If you are honest with yourself, you will admit that your hate and resentment have produced a headache, spoilt your appetite and robbed you of rest, made you unhappy and caused you to become a less desirable companion or friend. If, however, you refuse to hate or feel resentment and "turn on" all your batteries of love and forgiveness, you will cause healing currents to flow through every part of your body; you will become happier and a more desirable companion and friend. This does not mean that you are to cultivate weakness, far from it, for it takes a strong character to overcome hate by means of love.

Indulging in destructive thoughts produce, quite apart from any action, disastrous effects on the health. There are always numberless people who are always "out of health", who can never feel robust and radiant with health, who are frequently under the doctor's hands, or for ever swallowing quack medicines, whose lack of health is primarily due to the low character of their thoughts. The good forces of life are diverted into the wrong channels, simply by the indulgence in negative thinking. Allowing the mind to dwell upon thoughts of this kind, or attempting to distract themselves from them, causes repression with all its harmful results. If harmful thoughts are examined and the mind is 'cleansed' from their ill-effect, the good life forces flow freely into their right channels, producing normal health and vitality.

It is an equally well-known and established fact that one who gives way to worry can never be well. Some people are "born worriers". They inherit the condition and, not knowing any better, allow it to master them, thus destroying their health and happiness. Worry comes upon them in periods or waves. When these waves are encountered, they are hopelessly overwhelmed and submerged. They can neither sleep, nor digest their food, nor attend properly to their duties. Their health goes all to pieces and their efficiency is reduced fifty percent. After a few days of hell's torments, the wave gradually dies away and they find, as a rule, that their worry and fear have been groundless. Such people can never know what good health is. Their faces become lined, drawn and pinched by the strain of worry, and their expression proclaims them to be the hopeless victim of the "worry habit". They can never be cured of this until they learn thought-control and enter into the *truth*, which is, that, in a deep and spiritual sense, there is really nothing about which they need worry, because all things are working together for their good.

Worry is, of course, primarily due to fear. Fear is the worst enemy with which man has to contend. It is the greatest adversary of the metaphysical healer. The healer knows that it is not so much the malady itself, but *fear* that prostrates the patient. Nearly everyone is a victim of fear. It is deeply rooted in the human heart: fear of the future, fear of the unknown, fear of disease, fear of death, fear of failure, fear of poverty, fear of unemployment, fear of old age, fear of loss, fear of fate, fear of life itself. I have been through the painful experience of seeing those whom I have loved, literally and actually worry themselves into their graves – filled with every imaginable fear; yet, actually, there was nothing to fear.

Fear breaks down the nervous system and lowers the tone of the whole body and produces a morbid condition favourable to disease. Fear also magnifies the disease or ailment, for it affects the imagination and this causes all the inner powers of nature to reproduce in the body, the diseases pictured by the imagination.

Fear is based on error. There is no fear where truth reigns. One who knows the truth understands that there is nothing about which to be afraid, for in reality, all is well, and everything that comes into our life is good. Fear is based on the age-long, fundamental error that life is evil and is always eager and willing to do us an evil turn. Whereas the truth is that life is good in every particular and is always endeavouring to do us a good turn if possible.

People can be divided into two classes: those who believe life to be evil and those who believe it to be good. The latter enjoy a quiet, deep happiness which nothing can shatter. They possess a peace which no one and no circumstances can take away. Further, this peace, happiness and calm confidence make for health, for "in quietness and in confidence shall be your strength". One who can rest unafraid in the infinite, brings all the inner forces of nature into harmonious action. Because there is harmony and peace of mind and soul, it follows that there is harmony in the working and activities of the life processes of the body – thus making for improved health. People who belong to this class tend not to worry nor indulge in fearful thinking, because they *know* that everything is working together for their good and that of the whole. Theirs is a care-free (not *careless*) life. They have their troubles, difficulties and trials, but knowing the truth, *they do not magnify them*, neither do they oppose them. It is wonderful how much easier troubles and difficulties become if met in the right spirit. Still more remarkable is the good effect on the health, for instead of man being as "a kingdom divided against itself", and his life filled with discords and inharmonies, there is unity and wholeness. Man becomes one with life's purpose and aim, and in harmony with the great divine plan that is behind everything. Consequently, there is no opposition, no jangling, no disorder – only peace, order, cooperation.

Those, however, who regard life as inherently bad, and they compose the great majority of humans, find life very hard. Naturally, fear is their constant companion, for they do not know what blow life may deal them next. Being filled with fear, all the ills of life are greatly magnified; this, in turn, causes yet greater fear. Not only do they fear the real difficulties of life, they fear still more the imaginary ills – creatures of their imagination, which never materialise.

It is easy to understand what a tearing-down, destructive effect all this fear has upon the health and nervous system generally. It is easy to see how adversely the digestion, assimilation, and other vital processes of the body are affected, and how this interferes with nutrition; this, in turn, producing an impaired state of health and a lowering of tone that not only decreases efficiency, but lays the body open to disease and infection. This is bad enough, but worse is to follow.

Those who believe that life is 'evil' naturally oppose it. They oppose its discipline and its painful experiences. They believe that everything that is not pleasant is wrong, and therefore must be resisted. The unpleasant, unhappy experiences of life are, in reality, just as good as the pleasant and happy experiences. They all form part of a perfect plan which has for its object our highest good. Therefore, to oppose and rebel against the unpleasant experiences of life is to create terrible discord and disharmony. Unhappy is the one who attempts to oppose the forces and purpose of life. The one who batters his head against a stone wall is wise in comparison. *"A kingdom divided against itself cannot stand"*. And one who opposes life, thinking its experiences bad, creates a disruption which, only too often, is manifested in the life in the form of disease or ill-health.

Ill-health is largely caused by allowing the thoughts to dwell upon sickness and disease. If you are a careful observer of people's conversation you will notice that there is a type of person unlike the robust, cheerful, individual. You not infrequently meet them in railway carriages. Their conversation is entirely negative in character. You never hear them speak of overcoming, nor do they make any effort to look upon the bright side of life, or to raise their thoughts to higher and better things; they simply accept negative ills as a reality and think and talk from that point of view. On a recent railway journey, a party of women got into my compartment, and during the time we travelled about thirty miles, they never ceased to talk about illnesses, operations, ill-health, disease, sickness, deaths, funerals, hospitals, doctors and surgeons. Never once did they rise above this dreadful topic. It was obvious that their whole thought-life revolved round the subject of disease. If anyone had tried to get their thoughts on to higher levels, and speak of life, travel, the joy of living, of action, of achievement, they would, as quickly as possible, have brought the conversation back to the morbid but well-beloved subject of disease and sickness.

Any habit of mind that is morbid produces a morbid condition of body, and this results in lowered health and vitality, thus making one an easy prey to disease and infectious complaints. Especially destructive is the habit of brooding over the past, over the "what might have been". The past is dead: it can never be recalled, and we can safely leave it to an all-wise God who never makes any mistakes and who is able, always, to over-rule everything for good. If you have made mistakes in the past, brooding over them will not mend matters, but will make carrying out your present duties and responsibilities more difficult. If you have suffered severe bereavements, you will never forget those who have passed on, God forbid, but do realise that the Infinite One, who knows every detail of every life, and who fits everything together and makes out of it a complete and perfect whole, makes no mistakes, and that behind the blows of adversity is a perfect plan which some day you will see is for your highest good, and the highest good also of those from whom you are separated, only for a time. If you have wronged others in the past, do not brood upon your wrongdoing, for this does no one any good, and does actual harm to yourself. God is not only willing to forgive, but He is also able to work everything together for good, so that even the wrong that you may have wrought in the lives of others can be overruled in such a way as to become a useful discipline. No matter what the past may be, cease regretting it; above all, cease brooding over it. The past is dead, and is in God's wise keeping, and you can safely leave it with Him. It is possible for you to make a fresh start, to live a new life, and, by noble deeds and loving service, atone for the past. Lift your thoughts to higher things; occupy your mind with today's duties; refuse to think of the past and, instead, press on to a brighter future.

> "Every day is a fresh beginning,
> Listen my soul to the glad refrain,
> And spite of old sorrow and older sinning,
> And troubles forecasted and probable pain,
> Take heart with the morn and *begin again*".

It is often said that disease and sickness are due to 'sin'. Yes, but what sin? 'Sin' is simply in the thought, therefore hopeless, slack, negative thought is sin. There is no sin, judging by results, as great as thinking in this low, diseased, morbid fashion. It is dishonouring to God. Man's life is perfect as it is imaged in the divine mind, therefore man's diseases and sickness are due to a falling short, in thought, belief and outlook from the divine ideal. By thinking in this "diseased" manner, the good life forces are mis-directed in such a way as to produce disease, sickness and ill-health in the body. There is only one life, and this is divine, and therefore perfect, but man can, by his wrong thinking, cause this to manifest in "evil" form.

In contrast to the type of person just described, there are those who do not dwell consciously upon disease and sickness, yet they are strangers to health. Some of them, knowing the value of right thinking, may even try to guide their thoughts health-wards, yet they do not become healthy. In this case, the trouble is below consciousness. There is an inward spiritual disharmony and a clashing of spiritual forces which become translated into the outward life and in the body in the form of disease and ill-health.

There are those who believe that God specially afflicts them with disease, that they are specially chosen vessels who suffer as a special mark of divine favour. So long as they think this they will continue to suffer. A little thought would show them that a perfect creator cannot create imperfection. Such a thing is a philosophical absurdity. They, however, say that disease must be sent by God as a test, because it has such a good effect on the soul. It is true that the discipline of suffering is good for the soul, but this is because the Infinite One is able to work all things together for good. The universe and the lives of men are governed by immutable divine law.

By working against the law man produces very painful results: he has to suffer for every infraction, for all "falling short" from the Divine Ideal, and these sufferings are good for him because they teach him, in future, to harmonise with the law. He, however, is the cause of his own suffering, and the fact that he suffers does not prove that he is a specially favoured child of God.

The whole truth of the matter is that humans are designed to be perfect, but through wrong thoughts, ideas, beliefs, emotions and passions, we fall from, or come short of, the Divine Ideal, thus manifesting in our lives disease, sickness and other disharmony. The cause of our troubles is within ourselves. This is an unpalatable truth to some, but there is another side to the shield. If the cause of all our troubles is within ourselves, then there is a way by which they can be overcome, for, by becoming inwardly changed, our lives can, in turn, become correspondingly transformed. It was because of this great truth that our Lord insisted upon a complete inward change. *"Ye must be born again"* implies a complete reversal of thought. No longer must we think in terms of disease, sickness, ill health and other limitations, or indulge in hurtful thoughts, but we must think instead, in terms of infinite wholeness, health, life, purity, joy, love and peace, and in so doing we shall reconstruct our lives anew.

Within you is the power. The power to be well instead of sick. This power is divine, God-given - the very life of God, who is the *all-life*. It is yours *now*. You do not have to wait for a future state, the power is yours *here* and *now*, to use at this moment. You are free *now*, could you but believe it. God's power to heal has not lost its potency. One who will believe in the divine power within can rise to higher and better things, mount up with wings like an eagle, and live life on a higher plane, above negative ills and afflictions.

Chapter Two

Divine Healing

Instructions for those who Wish to be Healed

One of the most helpful aids to divine healing is to spend a few minutes before retiring in forgiving all who have ever wronged you in any way, and all against whom you may have any dislike or resentment. It may cause old wounds in your heart and affections to open: if so, it is good for this to be done, for no healing can take place until these old wounds have been thoroughly cleansed by divine love, and all who have injured you completely forgiven. Having forgiven them freely, send out your love to them, and tell them that you forgive them and that you love them. Now, as you lie in bed, drowsily waiting for sleep, say softly over and over again with a glad and thankful heart: *"Forgive me all my trespasses, even as I have forgiven those who trespass against me"*.

Let your last thoughts before sleeping be of love, forgiveness, harmony, peace and rest in the love and forgiveness of God.

Immediately upon waking, say several times:

"God is my life, my health, my strength, my all. Divine life is my life, my body is filled with its power".

During the day, when tempted to think or speak of yourself as sick or diseased, repeat the above words instead: endeavour to realise that you are perfect as imaged in the divine mind, and try to live in the consciousness of this great and glorious truth.

Try to avoid listening to other people's talk about disease, sickness and illness. Change the subject and get the conversation running into healthier channels.

Try always to think and speak of love, joy, health, brightness, progress, happiness, good will. Refuse to speak or think of anyone except to help them and try and get others to do the same.

Avoid fault-finding and running people down. Criticising other people, especially, should be avoided as you would the plague. Try, instead, not to see people's faults and failings, but make up your mind to see only good in them. Criticism is a great cause of ill health, and, by refusing to indulge in it, you will not only benefit your health, you will also find that people around you will change in a mysterious way and become more friendly, happy and harmonious.

Remember, your life is largely a reflection of your thoughts. Get your thoughts in harmony, first with the divine love, and second, raised up to the divine perfection. Do this and your ill health will vanish, and your life become transformed.

Hitherto you have been living in the consciousness of ill health and disease, just in the same way that one who is in constant poverty lives in a fixed idea of poverty, around which his thoughts continually revolve. What is continually held in the mind works out into the life and becomes externalised in the body. A fixed idea of poverty and limitation will so limit and control the whole of a person's actions, judgement and decisions, that poverty will always be their companion. In the same way a thought life that is lived in the consciousness of disease and sickness will also influence the body as to produce sickness and disease. The body is made-up of millions of conscious entities who obey the subconscious mind. This mind is influenced by your thoughts, by your dominant ideas, and by the consciousness in which you habitually dwell. If you live in a disease consciousness, then, the subconscious mind will act accordingly, and all the living, conscious entities in your body will faithfully labour to bring forth ill health or disease in your body. If you have been living and thinking in a consciousness of disease and ill health, you have been dishonouring God, who is perfect Wholeness, Life, Health, Purity and Good. If, therefore, you would be well, it is necessary that you raise your thoughts and feelings to this higher consciousness of God's Wholeness, Health, Life and Perfection. *In other words, think with God instead of against Him.* Persevere with this, continually raising your thoughts, and affirming joy, happiness, health, harmony, peace, love and other positive qualities of the Divine Mind, and you will find that you will, in course of time, become raised to a higher consciousness which will transform your health and your life.

Finally, remember that there can be no healing so long as you regard sickness, disease or ill health as evil, and therefore something to be feared and resisted. The first thing the healer has to do is to help the patient to realise that his pain and suffering are good and the manifestation of Infinite Love. Probably 90% of pain and suffering and actual disease and illness are due to mental tumult; to looking upon sickness and pain as evil and resisting them.

Henry Victor Morgan, the Healer-Poet, in his little book, *The Healing Christ*, says:

> This teaching of non-resistance of evil, the understanding that every experience is good if we thus approach it, is a mighty lever in the equipment of the healer.

You will find that as soon as you can convince the mind of the patient that all his trials have been periods of development, that every pain has been kindly in showing him that law has been disobeyed, this attitude of mind will have a marked effect in bringing relaxation to the body.

If called upon to treat a patient whose body is wracked with pain, and has become tense with resistance, fix your mind on them with intense realisation, saying: "Listen to me. You are destined to be in the image and likeness of God. Your old diseased body is dying daily, and your new body, created in the likeness of God, is being born."

The pain you are suffering is not an enemy, but a friend. It is the invisible surgeon assisting in clearing the way for the new body. You contemplate the perfect body and endure the suffering until it has done its perfect work.

In the joy of birth, you are free. As soon as pain *is recognised as kindly*, you have agreed with your adversary and the healing goes on apace.

If you resist pain the body becomes tense, the life current becomes impeded, and very often nature has to throw you into a fever in order to heal the hurt which is the child of your ignorance.

The true science of Jesus is embodied in: "*I say unto you resist not evil*", and again: "*agree with an adversary quickly, while thou art in the way*", for when you have ceased to resist evil, evil for you has ceased to be, and when you have agreed with your adversary, your adversary is transformed into an Angel with healing in his wings.

Again, T.J. Shelton in *The Scientific Christian* says:

> You recognise evil when you resist it. So, in order to heal your patient, you must teach non-resistance. When the patient is suffering with pain,

there is resistance; *that very resistance increases the pain* and gives power to evil (so-called).

"Resist not evil!" This is what the Lord Jesus tells you; it is a scientific statement. All science is practical Truth. Just get your patient to relax and let go, and evil ceases to be - it has no being in itself. All the power that it has comes from *your* thought, or that of your patient; it is your duty to correct the thought of your patient.

Endeavour always to realise that everything that comes into your life is due to the working of the infinite love. Everything that comes to you, no matter how stern the discipline, should be welcomed with open arms, as a friend and not as an enemy, for it is a friend, seeking to minister to your highest good and your internal joy. The fact that love has to manifest in the form of pain and sickness is not because it is not love in its very essence, but because you have opposed and obstructed it in the past, and because you have not learned certain lessons. Oppose the love no longer, but meet it with open arms, learning willingly the lessons life has to teach. This is the way to health.

Do not be dismayed or disheartened if you meet with setbacks. Those who set out to climb the steep heights, and to live a fuller and richer life, are generally tested and tried. This is the time when determination, resolution and faith are required. When all seems lost the battle is really won, for you are only being tested by the appearance of failure, in order to see if you are worthy of promotion to a higher plane of living.

When you are down in the valley, realise that behind it all is the Infinite Love. Endeavour also to realise that your life is perfect as imaged and created in the *divine mind*, and that this perfect image is the reality and all else is transient and unreal. Affirm, declare and endeavour to realise the perfection of the real YOU as imaged in the *infinite mind*. Keep raising yourself up to this divine ideal which is the reality - do this, and you will come safely through your adverse period, wiser and stronger for the experience.

Remember that everyone has to pass through adverse periods of trial and stress. By following the teaching of this little book, you will, however, be able to weather, safely, storms which, if you had continued in the old way, would have overwhelmed you and left you a wreck upon a desolate shore.

When you are well and things are going smoothly with you do not, on any account, allow yourself to slip back into the old ways. Every day spend a short time in *the silence*, that is, withdraw from the outer world of the senses and contact the inner ideal world of spiritual perfection, and realise that you, *the real you*, are perfect as imaged in the *divine mind*. Try to form a mental concept or picture, as well as you are able, of your highest conception of God's perfection, and realise your oneness with it. Realise, too, the *allness* of good and love and get into harmony with God's perfect law. Forgive all men, love all creatures - become at one with the cosmic scheme.

This is the divine way of health, harmony and happiness. Follow this, and you will gradually climb to a higher vibration, to a higher plane, where adverse influences will affect you but little.

It is a steep ascent, but you can "arrive" if you will follow Truth patiently and *never give up the quest*.

CHAPTER THREE

Thoughts and Health

God, who is perfect, can think only perfect thoughts, and can form only perfect ideas, therefore the human being also must be whole and perfect. But the perfect thought of God, what may be termed the *essential* or *archetypal human*, the true idea of God. That this true, essential, archetypal human does not manifest is due to the fact that we do not live our thought life on the same level. Instead, we think, move and have our being on a low level of consciousness, in which ill health, disease, and every form of negativity, are taken for granted and looked upon as a sort of reality. Because of this we manifest these dreadful things. Yet, if we did but live on the higher level and think, speak and act, and also feel from the standpoint of the *essential human*, then perfection would manifest instead of imperfection, to an ever-increasing degree.

People often say: "How can I think from the standpoint of health and wholeness and of overcoming, mastery and victory, while suffering from ill health, or associating with people who are suffering from disease?" This difficulty is a very real one, but it is helpful if we bear in mind at all times that real part of us, the only part of us that is real, is the *essential human*. If we persevere in this, we find ourselves thinking and acting from the level of truth, ie: that which is really true of the *essential human*. Thus, we grow into a new and higher consciousness. It is helpful also if we try to form some mental concept of the beauty and perfection of the *real archetypal human*.

> "The Father of all things brought forth [archetypal] Man, like unto himself, Whom he loved as His own Child; for he was beautiful beyond compare, having the image of his Father. In very truth God loved His own Form, and on him did this to all His own formations".
> From the Divine Pymander of Hermes Trismegistus

If we try to realise this truth about the true creation of Man, and bear in mind that it is the only thing about us that is really true, it makes a tremendous difference to our health, character and circumstances. Living in the consciousness of this truth makes it difficult for us to do an unworthy deed, or even to think an unworthy thought.

Instead of our mind dwelling upon limitation and imperfection we think in terms of Heaven and Infinite Good. The mind, being creative, brings forth that which corresponds to the type of our thought.

What is, however, easier is for some to think of the matter in this way: that we are indwelt by the Spirit of God. Saint Paul said: "Know ye not that ye are the temple of God, and that the Spirit of God dwelleth in you?" God Who indwells us is perfect. He is perfect life, health, wholeness and good. If we remember this at all times, and also reflect upon it, and think in terms of this transcendent truth, then what Jesus said: "Ye shall know the truth, and the truth shall make you free", becomes true in our experience.

> "And good shall ever conquer ill,
> Health walk where pain has trod.
> As a man thinketh, so is he;
> Rise then, and think with God".

Part 2: Power to Overcome

Overcoming Life's Difficulties

Hamblin Vision Publishing

CHAPTER FOUR

Foreword

BY W.G. HOOPER

I have been asked to write a foreword to this booklet, and this I do with pleasure. One of the greatest sages of ancient times wrote these words: *"With all thy getting, get understanding".*

It is not simply a knowledge of power humanity needs today as how rightly to use power on every plane of existence. A child may play with the explosive power of dynamite, but if ignorant of the laws of explosions, disastrous results would inevitably follow.

The whole universe, from centre to circumference, is full of energy and Power. But if that Infinite Power were not harnessed to Infinite Wisdom the universe would be chaos instead of a Cosmos.

Even so must the seeker after the power to conquer, to succeed, to become victorious in this life not only learn where power resides and how to use it, when he has discovered the secret, but he must also learn the secret of true wisdom; for apart from wisdom, power would be destructive to the highest interests of the evolving soul.

The Trinity of Divine Being is to be found in the Divine Will, Wisdom and Love, and these three must always go together before there can be perfect balance, perfect adjustment, in any state of life or existence.

As Mr Hamblin so wisely points out, the true key to spiritual power is to learn how to work in harmony with the divine will of the universe, for if the soul challenges that will, which is all love and all wisdom, then inevitably the soul will get hurt. We cannot break the universal laws of wisdom and love. Rather we get broken in the attempt to do so.

Knowing these cosmic truths, we search for the secret of real power and real strength, and all philosophers, sages, mystics and prophets unite in declaring that the source of that principle is within the soul, and not outside it.

It is alone in the consciousness of the divine self - that eternal reality hidden within - which lies at the back of human experience that the true secret of a power that is irresistible and all powerful is to be found.

Paul called this power the Power of Christ, as opposed to the dogmatism and selfish power of a humanity half animal and half human: *"Christ is the Power of God, and Christ is the Wisdom of God"*, declared this undaunted and heroic soul who had faced the shams and hypocrisy of the world of time and sense, and saw they were all elusive.

Further, he went on to declare that this power and wisdom are within the soul of man, and goes on to make the audacious statement that this mystery had been hidden for ages, and that he was one sent to teach the world that special message - which was: *"Christ in you, the hope of glory"*. By this he meant there was an eternal seed of divinity which included power, wisdom, and love in every soul, which through the ages had travelled the great path of involution and evolution.

Science today is confirming this truth of the marvellous inwardness of things, and of the wondrous power latent in the small and minute. The atom is now seen to be a centre of wondrous energy and force, yet the body is composed of millions of these very atoms. How to unlock their energy is the quest of the seeker. Paul had found it, for he affirms: *"I can do all things through Christ who strengtheneth me"*.

Every soul needs the consciousness of this indwelling something, call it by what name you will. The knowledge that by the dignity, courage and spirit within it, it can face and conquer the world of shams, hypocrisy and greed.

The artist, the painter, the musician, the writer, the mechanic, the miner, indeed, all workers who desire to climb the spiritual ladder to mastership, need this consciousness of a mighty invisible force behind and within their life.

The linking up of the life with the life universal, the wisdom that governs all things, and the love that rules the cosmic laws, is the only sure guide to the real pathway to power. Any other way leads to disappointment, failure and defeat.

Today I planted many kinds of seeds in my garden at Cranemoor. Each seed was a potential plant, nay scores of plants, with wondrous colours, fragrance, beauty and form involved. Within the seed they concealed, in germ form, all this formless glory. Yet it was there.

How to make that potency dynamic and alive was the problem. Yet how simple the solution. I had but to bring the seeds into harmony with the divine life of the universe, expressed in mother earth, the light of the sun, the electricity of the clouds, and the gentle rain, and lo! the problem was solved.

In effect I did very little, it was the Universe which was going to work on the germ in the seeds. The universal life speaks to the power hidden within the seed and says: *Wake up! Be alive. Put on a new robe. Burst thy bonds of matter, and let My Life, My Power, My Wisdom express themselves through you.* And they obey the law of life and love, and grow and beautify the garden, giving food and pleasure to every beholder.

It is even so with man. Man, the offspring of eternal power, the potential Son of God, the half animal and half Divine, in whose nature there lies buried the creative force of the infinite - to this dead soul - the universal life is speaking to-day. Arise! Shine, thy light is come! Wake up! For ages thou hast been asleep, buried in thy animal nature. Its senses and desires have enthralled thee, but, within thee, I dwell. I, the creator, the spirit of the universe, the moulder and fashioner of circumstance - the conqueror of time, the creator of destiny.

My presence, my power shall be with thee, my wisdom shall inspire thee, my love shall inflame thee, and out of the multitude that follow death and selfishness there shall be born a divine child, who through faith in the all-good has learned where the Kingdom of truth, of love, and life resides.

As I know that Mr Hamblin is able to express these principles of life, wisdom and love, I recommend readers earnestly to weigh up his words in this booklet and then to pass it on to others. The world needs truth today. Truth as it is in the eternal scheme of things. I know of no author who is presenting truth in a more simple and direct form than is the author of these series of booklets on "Power". The Blessing of the Spirit abide with them.

W. G. Hooper, F.R.A.S.[1]

Cranemoor
Highcliffe-on-Sea
Hampshire
England

---

1. W. G. Hooper, Fellow of the Royal Astronomical Society and author of **The Pathway of the Gods** and **The Universe of Ether and Spirit.**

Chapter Five

The Power is Within

This little book teaches that the power is within the individual and not in our circumstances. So long as we *think* that life is governed by our circumstances, we are dominated by them. This is due to the fact that our outward life is the result of our thoughts. So long as we think that the power of our thoughts is nothing, and that we are a victim of circumstances, we remain a pawn in the game of life: we are mere driftwood floating on the sea of life.

Man, in reality, is the creator of his own circumstances and environment, therefore they have no power in themselves but only the power with which he invests them by his thought. One often hears it said that a man of action does not wait for opportunities, but creates his own. This is perfectly true.

The strong man of action believes in his power to overcome difficulties and adverse circumstances, and, because he believes this, he accomplishes often the apparently impossible. Others, on the contrary, have no belief in their own power to overcome circumstances, believing, instead, that they are helpless victims of a malevolent influence. So long as they believe this, they must remain a helpless victim, for *"as a man thinketh in his heart, so is he"*.

As will be seen later, the overcoming of life's difficulties and circumstances is not accomplished by fighting them, but by learning the lessons of experience and working within the good purpose of life instead of against it.

While one woman or man is a strong and useful citizen because they believe in their own power to overcome difficulty and adverse circumstances, another is helpless, inefficient, and a drag on others because they have no belief in their own power to overcome circumstances, but believe, instead, in the power that environment has over them. The former helps along the progress of the race, serves their day and generation, and is an inspiration to others. The latter is a drag on the wheels of progress, has to be helped by other people, and is certainly no encouragement to others. We see by this that people either conquer their lives or are defeated, according to their mental attitude, habit of thought and type of belief. We see, also, how vitally important the attitude of mind and type of thought are, for by them we either unlock the power of the Infinite into our lives, or shut ourselves off entirely from its influence, making ourselves weak and helpless in the face of adversity.

The same truth can be put in other words by saying that people attract to themselves an environment of a certain type corresponding to their attitude of mind and soul. It depends entirely upon how they meet the difficulties and adverse circumstances of life as to whether they overcome or become submerged. Trouble does not destroy a person; it is giving into it that submerges them. If a human has no belief in the power to overcome life's difficulties, and if they think that circumstances and environment are stronger than them, they are defeated in advance. As soon as adversity comes, they give into it; or, even if they struggle, it is hopeless, for, having no belief in a power within them greater than their difficulty, they have nothing upon which to draw. Their poor, finite resistance is soon exhausted, and they are defeated by powers which, in a real sense, have no existence or vitality. What effect does this giving into difficulty have? Does it produce a better environment? It is not necessary to say that it does not. Every defeat leads downwards to the gutter and despair.

In the case of the other type, they, too, meet with difficulty and adversity, but they do not succumb. They believe that they can overcome, consequently they are stronger than their difficulties. Not only do they weather the storms of life, they also become stronger by so doing. In this case, each difficulty or adverse condition leads upward. Becoming stronger and more efficient through successful conflict and experience, they are able to condition their lives more after their deals.

We thus see that humans, first by thought and belief, and next by actions, either create their environment or attract it to them according to what belief it is that is held in their minds.

We see that the power is in us and not in our circumstances or environment: we see also that it depends on the type of thought and belief we hold as to whether we allow this power to flow into our life, or if we cut ourselves off from its help and influence.

The power is infinite, and, by coming into conscious identity with it, we can draw freely upon omnipotence. Instead of being poor, puny and weak, tossed to and fro by every wind of adversity, we find that there is no difficulty in life that cannot be overcome, no temptation that cannot be resisted, no height to which we cannot climb.

We have seen that a person who believes that they can overcome life's difficulties finds that they can do so. They may believe that they, the human, is overcoming, but in reality, this is not so. The power of the finite personality is limited and easily exhausted. What the strong person of achievement draws upon, although they may not realise it, is the Power of the Infinite.

This power does not become available unless it is believed in, called upon and made use of. Some people seem to do this naturally and unconsciously. They believe in a vague, subconscious sort of way that they have a power within them that is greater than their difficulties. That this power is spiritual, and that it is the Power of the Infinite made available by their faith in it does not occur to them. They simply believe in themselves, and what they think is their own power, and, because of this belief, faith and confidence, are able to achieve and conquer, not knowing that they're using a power greater than that of their finite personality.

If this simple faith in ourselves and in our ability to overcome the troubles and difficulties of life enables us to become victorious over adversity, how much more will this inward power become available if it is understood, consciously appropriated and relied upon?

The power is within you. It can be used for good purposes or bad. If used wisely, it builds up the life in harmony and beauty. If, however, it is used unwisely, it will produce suffering and disaster. It is the object of this little book to help people, not only to discover this power, but to use it wisely, in obedience to Immutable law, and in harmony with the divine purpose of life.

Humankind is emerging from the stage when, from the cradle to the grave, one is a mere puppet of circumstance, and many are now realising the greatness and potency of their interior powers.

If the Power of the Infinite is used wisely all will be well, but if it is used wrongly and against the laws of life and being, humankind will pull down civilization about its ears and destroy itself. Spiritual powers and the power of thought are so potent that nothing can withstand them. It is therefore of the utmost importance that people should be shown how to use these forces aright.

Chapter Six

The Life of Victory

No life can be absolutely smooth. All have their conflicts, their griefs, sorrows, disappointments, apparent disasters and adversities. Everything depends upon how we "take" life, and in what spirit we meet its difficulties. Life is a splendid experience and a glorious adventure to those who meet its discipline willingly and courageously. Those who overcome their difficulties and learn willingly its lessons, find that their life becomes deeper, richer and fuller as the years go by. Those, however, who try to avoid life's discipline, who seek an easier path, or who try to fight their battles in the feeble, shallow strength of their finite personality, lead lives which become an ever- increasing hell of trouble and torment. *"Do not pray for easy lives, pray to be stronger men",* wisely said Phillips Brooks. These are words of the ripest wisdom. They are a trumpet-call to the weak-kneed, bidding them join the conflict that is shared willingly by all true heroic souls.

This life is a training school. So long as man or woman thinks that it is merely an opportunity for having a good time, they walk in the darkness of ignorance, and, incidentally, creates for themselves endless trouble. No one can go through life without meeting with adversity. Adversity is necessary in order to discipline the soul and strengthen and build up character. If life were all smooth sailing, what flabby, useless creatures we should become! Discipline, adversity, difficulty and trouble are necessary in order to perfect us through experience. Therefore, life can never be easy and, what is of more importance, we cannot make it easy, no matter what we may do nor how we may try.

Every life is one of difficulty and adversity. To other people a person's life may appear to be placid, peaceful, and one succession of successes and triumphs. Outsiders, however, know nothing of the secret struggles, the overcoming, perhaps, of almost every kind of difficulty that has formed part of the life which, outwardly, appears to be so easy.

Life must have its difficulties and adversities. If, however, they are met and overcome, life increases in splendour, and all difficulties become easier by comparison, because of one's increasing strength. The greater and more numerous the difficulties that are overcome, the stronger the conquering soul becomes, consequently, the easier life and its difficulties appear to be. On the other hand, one who runs away from life's discipline or who fails in his efforts to overcome its adversities, becomes weaker, and the weaker he becomes, the greater life's difficulties appear to be. Thus, we see that one who overcomes, enters a life of ever-increasing splendour and joy, while the one who fails to overcome has to live a life of increasing misery and failure.

Everyone, then, has his troubles, setbacks, failures, difficulties, adversities, and the success or otherwise of his life entirely depends on how he meets them. Shall he be submerged by trouble, adversity, difficulty or disaster, or shall he overcome and become a conqueror in the strife? It is utterly impossible to escape from, or avoid, life's discipline. Life's lessons must be learned, and if we try to avoid them, our difficulties and sufferings repeat and increase until we do learn them. This is all due to the working of Immutable Law, which never varies a hair's breadth and which, of course, cannot be evaded.

We must meet our difficulties. How, and in what way, shall we meet them? Shall we go under, or shall we become a conqueror? We have already seen that it depends entirely upon how we meet them as to whether our life shall be a triumph or a terrible failure. It is seen, then, that while we are victims of fate to the extent that we must meet with difficulties, and, at times, adversity, yet we can make our lives either a triumph or a failure by the way in which we meet our troubles.

Said Phillips Brooks: *"Do not pray for tasks equal to your powers: pray for powers equal to your tasks"*. In these fine words this inspiring writer again gets to the very roots and foundation of all true success in life. There is, indeed, no cause for failure. The life of overcoming and victory is possible to those who will meet life's difficulties with a high courage, calling upon the Infinite Power within for all their needs. There is no limit to the power within, for it is inexhaustible: the only limit that can be placed upon it is the limitation imposed by doubt and fear.

To sum up: we see that life cannot be made easier: that there is no such thing as having an easy time: and that life is a discipline and not a "joy ride". Yet we can become so strong, through overcoming, that life appears to be easy by comparison. Life, in itself, does not become easier, but we become so strong that life becomes easier to us. On the other hand, by failing to overcome life's difficulties, through trying to avoid life's discipline, and through failing to learn life's lessons, we become weaker and less able to overcome. Because of this our difficulties loom larger than ever, also the painful experiences which seek to teach us life lessons, repeat and become more acute, so that we have to learn through suffering and bitter experience that which could have been learned through overcoming and victory.

What is your attitude towards life? Do you know the joy of victory and overcoming, or are you failing in life and turning it into a hell of suffering and disappointment? This intense joy, which comes to the emancipated and free, may be yours if you will meet life in the right spirit, learning to overcome through the Power of the Infinite. You possess the power, but you cannot make use of it unless you recognise it and consciously identify yourself with it.

Within you is the power.

CHAPTER SEVEN

Lions in the Path

People often naturally think that the difficulties of life can only be overcome by resisting them. They think that discipline and trouble are evil and must be fought tooth and nail. They believe that there is some malignant evil which dogs their footsteps, seeking always to rob them of happiness and to upset all their plans. But the illumined know better. It has been revealed to them that life is good: that everything coming into the life is good, and that all trouble, trial and difficulty are but necessary discipline having for its object the highest good of the individual.

Until we understand the deeper things of life, we naturally think life is simply an opportunity for having a good time, and resent very much all those circumstances, difficulties and troubles which disturb our happiness. When, however, we enter a larger and more expanded consciousness and are able to look at life from the point of view of eternity or endless living, we see things in their true perspective and at their true value. We then see that we are beings of immense possibilities: that we are gods in the making: in our real selves, literally a son of God. We understand, then, that we are not an earthly creature at all, but a spiritual being, a son of God, undergoing a training or apprenticeship.

When life is looked at from this standpoint, that which in the old "sense" consciousness appeared to be evil is now seen to be a valuable discipline, preparing the embryo god for higher service and greater responsibilities.

It will readily be seen, then, that the reason life's discipline cannot be avoided is because behind it is the Infinite Love. It is Love that compels the learning of life's lessons, because of the great future in store.

The first great truth the student has to learn is that life, its purpose, its painful experiences and difficulties are not evil, but are, in reality, infinitely good and kind.

The second is that life's discipline cannot be avoided, and that if an attempt is made to do so the experience will be repeated again and again, each time becoming more severe and painful until the lesson is learnt.

The third is that life's experiences are not so very dreadful after all, if they are met in the right spirit. Every soul must meet with griefs, bereavements and disappointments; but these, if met rightly, have a mellowing influence, so that the character becomes enriched and strengthened and greatly improved as the years go by.

It is not the lessons which have to be learnt in this life that are the cause of man's suffering, so much as his resistance to life's discipline, and his fear of what life may bring to him next. I estimate that only a comparatively small percentage of man's suffering is inevitable, the remainder being the result of resistance.

Therefore, while it is true that life's discipline cannot be avoided, and that its lessons must be learnt, it is yet equally true that the greater part of man's troubles and sufferings, being self-created, can be overcome.

Chapter Eight

From Victory to Victory

We have already seen that not only is it impossible to fight fate successfully, for by so doing we fight against all the powers of the universe, but that to attempt to do so is greatly to increase our difficulties. We have also seen that fear also adds greatly to our sufferings. The higher the type of human being, the greater the ability to suffer. This is due to the fact that suffering is almost entirely mental. Fear stimulates the imagination and increases suffering a hundredfold. It is not, however, altogether a matter of mental suffering or the working of the imagination, for events and experiences, if the discipline of life is opposed, actually repeat themselves in the life, each time becoming more painful.

It is therefore obvious that's life's difficulties cannot be overcome by fighting them: how, then, shall we overcome our troubles instead of intensifying them?

First, it is obvious we must cease to oppose the Divine Purpose of our life. Call it fate, if you prefer.

Secondly, we must cease to fear what life may bring in the way of discipline and experience.

Thirdly, we must find out the purpose of life, and work with it instead of against it.

We must cease to fight life, because to do so is to smash ourselves up. We must cease to fear life, because there is nothing to fear. We must work in harmony with the motive and purpose of his life, for only by so doing can its inharmonies be overcome.

It is largely a matter of belief. If man believes that the purpose of life is evil, he will not only fear it but he will also either oppose its discipline or endeavour to avoid it. If, however, he believes that the purpose of life is good, he will no longer fear it, there being nothing to fear, neither will he seek to avoid its discipline, but will meet it with open arms, as a friend to be welcomed instead of an enemy to be shunned.

Not only is it necessary to believe that life is good, but it is necessary to think from this standpoint of truth, and to live in the light of its revelation. The difference between right and wrong thinking is, that whereas a "right thinker" believes life to be good, and continually thinks from this standpoint, the "wrong thinker", believing life to be evil, constantly thinks and lives in the belief that the purpose of life is evil and sinister.

It is not possible, at first, to enter into the realisation that the purpose of life is not evil but good. It is possible, however, for the student to hold firmly to the belief that life is good, and to train himself to think from this standpoint. This is "right thinking", which, if persevered with, will lead to realisation, which is a true spiritual illumination, by which man is able to know instead of merely to believe.

The central thought, the dominant note of life, must be the *"allness of good"*. A thousand doubts will assail the student, while the so-called "practical" experiences of life and inherited and inbred beliefs and early upbringing will all be against his new concept of life. The seeker after a fuller life will be tested and tried in every possible way, and if it were not for the power of the Spirit within him, he would utterly fail.

The inward power of the Spirit must never be misused in an endeavour to alter the outward life, for to do so is to create disasters of the greatest magnitude. This inward power may, however, be called upon to an unlimited extent, as a source of strength to sustain one in times of stress and trial. This inward spiritual power, while it must never be used for the overcoming of other people, can and should be used for the overcoming of self, and the building up of character.

Sustained, then, by an inward power that becomes greater the more it is called upon, it is possible for the student to pursue "right thinking" in spite of opposition and every form of discouragement. He thus comes into harmony with the inner purpose of life. Instead of fighting and resisting life's discipline: instead of fearing what each day may bring forth, he meets life's changes and experiences with open arms, recognising in them friends who have come to bless, rather than enemies who seek to destroy. Instead of turning his life into an inferno of unnecessary trouble, friction, discord and suffering, he reduces these things to their minimum.

It all depends upon how we look at life: what we believe, how we think and act, and how we make use of the inward power of the Spirit. One who will work along the lines laid down in this book will find that the majority of their difficulties will disappear like morning mist before the rising sun. The causes having been removed, the effects fail to appear. Life will not be without its testing times and griefs and disappointments, but, sustained by the invincible inward power of the Spirit the student will come through these strengthened, enriched and mellowed by experience. Thus, passing from victory to victory, the student finds that he or she can overcome all the difficulties of life, and, at the end, be satisfied with the use he has made of its opportunities. Then they will realise, even if they have not done so before, that life is very good: that each purpose is good: that each discipline is good, and that all things work together for good.

Part 3: Power to Succeed

How to create a successful life with the power of thought

Hamblin Vision Publishing

CHAPTER NINE

The Pathfinder

FOREWORD BY JOHN R. TODD

Whenever I think of the life story of Henry Thomas Hamblin I am reminded of a certain figure to be encountered in every chapter of the story of our race. This figure is the Pathfinder. He is present in every generation and in every department of the life of the planet. Science, art, commerce, government, industry, philosophy, research and religion, all are able to point to their pathfinders - men who have moved forward a little in advance of the main body of pilgrims journeying to their respective promised lands.

The Pathfinder is a lonely - sometimes, a pathetic - figure, for invariably, he is responding to an inward urge or call which has come to him, in particular, and singled him out to be the pioneer of some new enterprise, the investigator of some hidden thing, the explorer of some unknown hinterland.

I am aware that the author would be the last to claim for himself the distinction of a Pathfinder. The responsibility for my analogy is mine alone. Nevertheless, he is the pioneer of the Science of Thought Movement in this country; and prior to arriving at this phase of his career his lot had been closely akin to that of the lonely Pathfinder. His life, as I know it, has been a solitary seeking for, and an earnest striving after, that elusive thing or condition we call success - which he has been led to make the subject of this little book.

Despite the fact that there is a considerable literature on the subject, there is room for this booklet. The topic is a big one and it is many sided. It is almost impossible to pin it down with one brief definition to meet all needs. For example, success is one thing to the novelist, another to the philosopher, another to the business-person and yet another to the uncultured savage of Celebes. Each one visualises success as he is - it is a condition of individual phases. Wealth, Knowledge, Power, Fame and Pleasure, all may be ingredients in Success - yet none is the thing itself!

Henry Thomas Hamblin has touched success at more than one point. Let me indicate one phase in particular. With a scanty education, no money, no influence, feeble health, and amidst the fierce competition of modern life, he achieved a substantial business success. Yet he came to see that a successful business, with its concomitant, the making of money, was not really *complete* success for *him*. By thinking, seeking and suffering, by pursuing a long, lonely trail, Henry Thomas Hamblin found at last that success for him was something greater and more solid than a prosperous business career and the accumulation of money. It was revealed to him at last, that true success is a spiritual, undying, eternal thing - a something which belongs, not to one phase or department of life, but to all that is meant by life itself.

In this little booklet, the true, inward meaning of success is placed before the reader. It is the outcome of the author's own experience - an experience strenuously and painfully obtained. That he is a safe guide I can claim with the assurance of my own personal knowledge. At different times I have been privileged to read some hundreds of letters from students of his teaching and readers of his books testifying in grateful and glowing terms to the practical help and guidance received.

Henry Thomas Hamblin lived his later life in retirement, devoting his life to the Science of Thought movement, and conducting its teaching, writing its books and editing *The Science of Thought* [1] magazine. This booklet is only one of many, written in similar strain, telling of the wonderful achievements possible to those who learn to rely, not on themselves, but upon the divine power within them [2] - to the breaking of all bonds, to the arising from all degradations and to the accomplishment of that true, whole, complete success which makes man one with the supreme wisdom, love and power that shapes the destiny of the human race.

---

1. A quarterly magazine is still published by the Hamblin Trust, now called **Hamblin Vision. Copies are available at** www.thehamblinvision.org.uk

2. *Within You is the Power* is Henry Thomas Hamblin's seminal work on this subject.

John R. Todd

CHAPTER TEN

What is Success?

It is not given to all to occupy high positions or to achieve fame, but it is possible for each one of us to be truly successful in the work for which we are most suited, and which is our true sphere of labour. To one is given one talent: to another five, and so on. We are each called to different service, and for each one of us there is a niche in life which no one else can fill. Some follow trade, others the arts or the professions, but whichever or whatever it is, there are difficulties to be overcome.

It is difficult to define success, for the word does not mean quite the same to any two people. However, although success to one may be quite a different thing from what it may mean to another, there is yet one broad definition which will apply to all. In this wider sense, success means accomplishing in life something that is really worthwhile. It may also be described as being "top dog", not over other people, but over life generally.

Conquering and Achieving

This implies conquering, overcoming, achieving, so that when the life is finished there is honest cause for satisfaction. It is "up to us" all to do something with our life, and to make something of it. It is not meant that we should be drifters and failures, but that we should overcome life's difficulties, stem the current, and arrive at a destination. Success is not the "piling up" of wealth, or the achievement of selfish aims, but is the doing of something in life that is really worthwhile, that enriches the world and adds to the common good. Success and achievement of this kind bring no regrets or remorse but add happiness to the life and satisfaction in the hour of death.

Success is not due to outside circumstances, to chance or to fate. It is not altogether the fruit of ability, for the cleverest people often fail to make a success of their life, neither is it due very much to heredity or influence, although all these things may be useful.

The Three Fundamentals of Success

Success is due chiefly to three things: faith, vision and service. First, there must be faith in one's power to win, for without this success is impossible. If a man has no faith in himself he is, indeed, in a poor way, and no success can ever come to him. All who would be successful in their calling must have faith in their power to succeed. They must be so convinced of this that no failure or setback can ever shake their confidence. One who would succeed must have such faith in their power to succeed that even though the whole world be against them, they will remain undaunted. People who are really successful may know nothing of the greater power within them, but, instinctively, they believe in it, call upon it and make use of it. There are two kinds of belief in oneself. There is the belief or conceit of the fool in his own pretended abilities, who thinks that he is competent to do things which are entirely beyond his capacity. Superficial egotists of this type believe in their shallow selves and become so puffed up with pride they cannot see their own limitations. There is also the faith of the strong and able person, who believes, not so much in their abilities, as an inward strength that is greater than their finite powers. Such a person knows their own limitations and trusts a *something* that they do not perhaps understand, but which they know is there and can be relied upon.

This belief in an inward power to overcome and achieve is really the real inner secret of a successful person's achievement. It is what distinguishes him from the ordinary individual who is never able to get above the dead level of mediocrity.

Chapter Eleven

Faith

Faith, either in one's inner powers or ability to win through, which amounts to a belief in the power within, is the secret of achievement and the essential fundamental of success. One who is possessed of a faith such as this can laugh at the storms of life. No matter how often they may taste the bitterness of failure - and what successful person does not, at times - they will rise again, and, profiting by experience, build up a greater success than ever before. Faith is as much necessary in mundane affairs as it is in the conflicts of the soul. Without faith it is impossible for us to be successful in life, we are bound to go down before its storms and difficulties. People without faith, when knocked down by adversity, fail to rise again. They cease trying, and join the ranks of those who, having let the golden opportunities of their life go by, talk of the success that ought to have been theirs, if only certain things had not happened.

Faith and courage are vitally necessary to all who would make something of their life and be of some use in the world. Success is not won without a struggle; high achievement is not possible except as the result of sustained effort. Unfortunately, many people expect a path of roses, thinking that they can proceed through life without failures, disappointments, and setbacks. This is impossible. All successful people have their failures and dark hours, when everything seems lost. All are tested and tried to the uttermost. The difference between those who succeed and achieve and those who fail and accomplish nothing, is not in opportunity and experience, but in the manner with which the adversities of life are met.

Faith and Success

The person of faith and courage learns lessons from his or her failures, makes a fresh start, and, profiting by painful experience, builds a more stable and enduring success. The person of little faith, on the contrary, fails to rise above the calamity, refuses to learn the lesson that it would teach, and never tries again. Instead of acknowledging that the cause of failure is within themselves, and endeavouring to remedy it, they blame circumstances and other people, pitching themselves as injured and ill-used by life and other people. Self-pity is the most destructive of all negative practices, and effectually blocks the path to all progress and achievement. One who pities himself acknowledges, by so doing, that he is a failure, and that circumstances are too strong for him. By pitying himself, he shows that he has no faith in a power within him that is greater than his circumstances.

Faith and Failure

This is very often the sole secret cause of failure. Some people have no faith, because they have nothing in which to believe. Let such realise that they have a power within them that is the one infinite omnipotent power. If they will do this: if they will call upon it and trust in it, they will find out there is no difficulty that cannot be overcome, no disaster that cannot be retrieved, no failure that cannot be made a stepping stone to a far greater success than was ever before dreamed possible. All our limitations are due to our doubt and fear, our lack of belief in the power within. We limit the illimitable by our thoughts, by our lack of faith and by our limited outlook. We have the Infinite to draw upon, and if we will but realise this we will find that "all things" are possible.

Chapter Twelve

Vision

Achievement of anything really worthwhile in life not only demands faith, it also requires vision. All other things being equal, the man of greatest achievement is always the man of largest vision. One of small outlook who visualises petty things can never achieve great things. In the same way the achievements of one whose vision is large can never be petty or small.

Man's achievements are always a reproduction of his vision or thought pictures: that is, of course, if he has the faith and courage to carry things through to a successful conclusion. What is held in the mind gradually works itself out into the life. The pictures of the mind, if constantly dwelt upon, become reproduced in everyday life.

All outward achievement is the result of inward vision. *"First in the unseen then in the seen"*, is a law of the universe. Things are first created in "mind stuff" before they can be produced or reproduced in the material, outer world. Gaze at a cathedral or a mighty bridge, and you see but the outward expression of the vision that was held in the mind of the architect or engineer.

Look also at a beautiful and noble life, and you see the outcome of beautiful and noble thought-pictures and lofty vision.

Mental Imagery

Vision is the most wonderful faculty that we have. By it, all the invisible forces of our life become focused and one-pointed towards a definite achievement. By it, all our actions become unconsciously directed towards the same goal. By it, the over ambitious man becomes caught up by powers which are greater than himself and forced into a position of burden and responsibility, which make him literally a slave. He finds, then, that no wealth or fame can compensate him for the loss of leisure, health, and the simple pleasures of life. In the midst of his success and fame his heart is sick with longing for a simpler and happier life. Alas, this has become impossible; he is suffering from the result of his over ambitious vision and mental imagery.

Vision is the greatest power of the human mind. Whatever is held in the mind, in the form of mental imagery, in course of time works out into the life. If, therefore, the mental pictures are of a wrong kind, how great must be the disasters wrought in the life. There is a divine purpose behind each life, a plan that is infinitely good. If the mental pictures are in harmony with the purpose of life, true success and achievement follow.

The Misuse of Mental Forces

If, however, there is a clashing between the two, the only possible result is extreme unhappiness, and what may appear, outwardly, to be success, may, in reality, be a terrible failure. In the early stages of the new life, this divine purpose and guidance may not be discernible, but a good substitute is to follow the highest ideals and the loftiest aims, as they appear to the soul at the time. If you follow the highest and loftiest aims you cannot go far wrong, and later, you will receive more definite guidance. (These ideals should, of course, be practical.)

Through misusing his mental forces, man can literally smash up his life. By visualising wealth, for instance, and willing very strongly that wealth shall come to him, he sets in motion powerful forces which become an irresistible power in his life, sweeping him off his feet and tossing him about like a shuttlecock. Wealth comes, if he is sufficiently strong in concentration and will, but with it disaster, grief, ill health and misery indescribable. Further, in order to realise his ambition he may sacrifice his home life and all its simple joys, the companionship of those whom he loves, until at last, having realised his ambition, he sits amid the ruins of his happiness, a despairing, disillusioned and broken-hearted man.

Mind Pictures

It is necessary to use this power of vision, for it is impossible either to tidy up the home or build a hen-coop without it.

What is necessary is that we hold in the mind pictures that are in harmony with what our intuition tells us is the highest and best. Instead of selfish aims after a surfeit of the things that perish - wealth, power, luxury, fame, there should be desires for a simpler, less selfish and more natural life, combined with service to others. This word service brings us to our next point, but before we pass onto it, it is necessary to say something about purpose, steadfastness and persistence.

Mental vision, to be effective, must be continuous. That is to say, if one picture or ideal is held in the mind for a time and then got tired of and replaced by another, nothing of any value will ever be achieved or manifested. If a man makes up his mind to build a hen-coop he must keep a vision of hen-coop in his mind until he has got together the tools and material and constructs the thing he desires to make. If, however, he holds a picture of a hen-coop in his mind for one day and then changes it for one of an eight-day clock, and the next day, for that of a bookcase, it will be seen that nothing tangible will ever result.

Constant Visioning

In the same way, if we decide to spring-clean a room downstairs, and, before this mental picture can materialise, alter it to one of a room upstairs, and then before anything definite is accomplished, decide to go out for a walk, it is obvious that results will be of negative character. It is the same with the larger affairs of life. There must be the steadfast mind, the sticking to the main purpose, the refusal to be drawn aside from one's endeavour. The vision must be constant and, if this is maintained, definite achievement in life will follow.

It will be seen, then, that the circumstances of life are largely the result of mind-picturing or vision. While it is true that over-ambition and selfishness and the picturing of wealth, fame and power, produce unhappiness and misery, it is equally true that the fear pictures of failure and disaster, bring also their corresponding outward manifestation.

Picturing Failure

Those who are forever visualising their own failure can never succeed in any undertaking. Their mental pictures of failure and disaster unconsciously influence their conduct, actions and judgement so as to produce these negative states. Picturing failure and poverty will produce them in the external life, therefore those who are naturally prone to this negative practice must reverse their mental pictures and bring them more into line with truth. The infinite knows no poverty or failure, such things have no place in the divine mind. We must raise our thoughts and vision more in accordance with the real truth of things.

Finally, true success can come only through service. The greatest among us must be willing to serve the least. All success is really based on service, although few suspect it.

Chapter Thirteen

Service

If our occupation is of no service to the community, it languishes and dies out. When a person's methods become obsolete, they cease to serve effectively, consequently, they are superseded by competitors who are more efficient and who, in consequence, serve the community better. A desire to serve others must always form the basis of all true success. It is a basic law of life which cannot be evaded. It is because people think that life can be tricked and success won without service, that makes them indulge in sharp practice or actual dishonesty. The end justifies the means, so they think. But the end they have in view is selfish possession of wealth, position or power, not service to the community. Because their aims are wrong, their actions are crooked. They seek to batten on the community instead of serving it; to rob it instead of adding to the common good.

The Law of Service

Such people go against the law of service and come to grief, so that we see people of splendid strength and intellectual and business abilities - people who, if they had served, could have climbed to the highest positions and received the greatest honours - come crashing down to ignominy and shame. It is true that not all crooked business and public figures get sent to prison, but if they can escape human law they cannot evade the higher spiritual law of sowing and reaping. *"Whatsoever a man soweth, that shall he also reap"* is forever true.

Faith, Vision and Service

We see, therefore, that all three things are necessary in order to achieve real and lasting success. First, faith, because it connects us with the Infinite and brings the power of the illimitable into action. Second, vision, because it gathers all the invisible powers of the mind into the required channel, focusing them and making them one pointed. This, in turn, affects every action, turning it towards success and achievement, instead of failure and inefficiency. Third, service. He that is greatest must be the servant of the least. All the powers must be directed towards serving life and the world instead of self. Let the little-minded and those of small achievement or none take heed of this. Those of great achievement, those who bear the greatest burdens of responsibility would never continue if it were not that they realise that they are servants of the public. If they consulted their own comfort and feelings, they would retire into private life and enjoy a well- deserved rest and some of real joys and happiness of life. It is their public spirit and their desire to serve, that enable them to keep on.

No Success Without Service

There can be no success without service. Selfishness can never lead to true success, but only to disappointment and utter misery. Yet even here the law of service operates, for those who seek success from the lowest motives, must serve the community in some way, otherwise they can make no progress. Those who seek "big business" must put integrity and good service into their goods if they are to retain the confidence of the public. They must be sincere and honest in their efforts, otherwise the public will not support them. The same law applies to every calling and even to those who have no calling. All who would make their life a success must serve others.

It is necessary to emphasise again and again the necessity of work and service, for there are thousands who expect to win success and enjoy prosperity without either earning or deserving them. There is a quantity of so-called "success literature" circulating which teaches that both success and wealth can be obtained by mental magic instead of by ability, efficiency and service. Never once do these writers mention the word 'work'. Collectively, they number their followers by the tens of thousands, but I have never yet heard of one being benefited. Many of these writings teach what is merely a thinly veiled sorcery, and, unfortunately, such teaching is very attractive to the ignorant. All who practise the dark arts, be they teacher or student, it makes no difference, are bound to come to grief sooner or later. There may be apparent success for a time, but ultimately disaster overtakes them.

Failure is bound to follow practises that go against the law of service. All who seek to achieve success by mental magic are trying to take something, giving nothing in exchange. Because of this, they must, sooner or later, come up against spiritual law. No matter how sharp one may be, and no matter what methods may be employed, all attempts to obtain success or wealth without gaining it by merit and by fair exchange are bound to end finally in failure.

Further, all attempts to gain wealth or success without service, no matter whether it be by prayer, or "entering the silence", or picking a pocket, or floating a bogus company, or robbing a bank, are dishonest. One method is, in reality, as dishonest as another.

To endeavour to obtain wealth or to win success by mental magic is not an indictable offence, while to falsify a balance sheet or rob a bank is; but there is a higher Court of Justice than that of man, and this sees no difference between the two offences. There is a Law of Compensation which adjusts matters with absolute justice and impartiality. Whatsoever a man soweth, that shall he also reap, and life and the divine principle of absolute justice demand of each one a square deal. If we endeavour to get anything, no matter how small it may be, and not give our highest and best service in exchange, we have to square the account in another and more painful way. It is utterly impossible to get something for nothing, for no matter how much we may appear to gain on the surface, actually we lose, for we have to pay far more in other ways.

Cosmic Law and Principle

One who will not serve must suffer, and their sufferings will continue until they learn the great lesson of the square deal. This does not mean that those on meagre incomes are to give their means away and cast themselves on the tender mercies of an unsympathetic world. Instead, all can serve others to the best of their ability and to the limit of their strength and thus *square the account*. For everything that we receive we must give full value in service. It is far better to give ungrudgingly *first*; for, said the Great One, *"it is more blessed to give than to receive"*.

Chapter Fourteen

The Way of Real Success

To achieve anything really worthwhile in life, it is necessary, then, to believe in and have faith in the power within: to make use of vision, the creative power of imagination: to aim, not at selfish ambition, but highest service to life and the world. This will probably not lead to wealth, although, of course, it may do, but it will lead to satisfaction, content and happiness. It will bring into the life those things that wealth cannot purchase. Ella Wheeler Wilcox[1] truly says:

---

1. **Ella Wheeler Wilcox** (November 5, 1850 – October 30, 1919) was an American author and poet. Her works include the poem "Solitude", which contains the lines "Laugh, and the world laughs with you; weep, and you weep alone." Her autobiography, *The Worlds and I*, was published in 1918, a year before her death. (https://en.wikipedia.org/wiki/Ella_Wheeler_Wilcox)

> "Then give to the world the best you have,
> And the best will come back to you".

One who believes in the power within unconsciously calls upon it and brings it into action. If they apply this power in the way described here, they find that achievement is comparatively easy and responsibility light. Other people wonder how it is that they succeed so easily and bear so lightly the burden of their responsibilities. If, however, this power is used for selfish ends and self-aggrandisement, the results are disastrous. Every evolved soul is tempted in this way, and woe to the one who succumbs. If the inward, spiritual power is misused, it literally smashes the life up.

The Misuse of Inward Powers

Even more destructive is it to use, or rather, misuse, the inner powers for selfish ends. There are many writers today who are teaching their unfortunate victims to visualise "what they want" for half an hour at a time twice a day and to "will" it to come to them. Particularly, are they taught to visualise money and wealth and "will" it to materialise. This is the misuse of spiritual power against which every true teacher of hidden things has warned their followers.

Nothing worth having can be had without effort, and success cannot be won without paying the price. While the ordinary rank and file are wasting their time by killing time, the future executive and leader of men is studiously preparing himself for greater responsibilities. There must be a definite aim towards a well-defined goal, after which all the powers of the whole of the mind must be focused upon reaching the goal, principally, through becoming so competent and efficient and so faithful in service that it is obvious to everyone, especially those "higher up", that you are the very person, in fact, the only person, to fill the higher position.

You must be able to supply the world with something that it wants. They will pay handsomely if you can supply them with "something better". There is plenty of room at the top; it is only at the bottom of the ladder where crowds are trampling one another to death.

No one can climb the ladder who makes no effort to improve themselves and become more efficient. As you grow in character, efficiency and capacity, so will you find yourself higher up the ladder. If an inefficient individual finds himself, by some freak of fortune, higher up the ladder than his abilities deserve, the winds of adversity speedily blow him down again. Once get above the crowd, deservedly, and you will find your task fairly easy, for there is plenty of room. Those higher up are calling for efficient, capable people of steadfast character *and cannot find them*. The business world and other professions and callings are in need of people of vision, capacity, efficiency, who are capable of faithful service. Such people are very rare and difficult to find.

Unselfish Success

There is nothing selfish or mercenary in success based upon service and efficiency that comes to a person because they deserve it, for the more successful they are, the more efficiently and faithfully they serve others. One who serves in this way is never adequately rewarded monetarily, for such service can never be paid for either in wealth or honour. Therefore, if you are ambitious and willing to bear responsibility, fix your eyes on a definite goal and then by the exercise of faith and vision and by service make yourself fit to occupy a larger sphere of usefulness.

The winds of adversity will often try to blow you off the ladder, but if you have climbed by merit and if your faith is strong, you could never be moved, except to go up higher.

Remember, there is plenty of room higher up. Remember also that progress is comparatively easy once you have overcome initial difficulties.

Finally, at all times have faith in the power within you, for this will enable you to weather the fiercest storms of life. Keep the vision of your goal constantly before you and all the inner forces of your being will become focused upon its attainment. See to it that your aim is noble and within the range of reasonable achievement.

Part 4: Power to Transform Life

A Thought Revolution

Hamblin Vision Publishing

Chapter Fifteen

Preface

by Henry Thomas Hamblin

We all possess the power to transform our lives, but not all of us have the wisdom that is necessary. A great scientist once said that we can only conquer nature by obeying her. It is equally true with life; we can only overcome it and transform it, by unity and cooperation, in place of disunion and opposition.

There are certain laws of being which must be obeyed: there is also a purpose in life with which we must co-operate, if our life is to be changed from discord and unhappiness to harmony and peace.

This little booklet will endeavour to teach you the inner secret of successful living. Its message will appear to be foolishness to all whose eyes have not yet begun to open to hidden things; but those who are becoming spiritually awakened will find in it the only way out of their troubles, disharmonies and difficulties, and an entrance to a larger, fuller, and more abundant life.

The wisdom of the spirit is always foolishness to the unillumined human mind; but it is the only way by which man can find a way out of the perplexities and chaos of his life.

Until man is willing to be led and guided by a wisdom and intelligence greater than his own, there can be no end to his difficulties and perplexities. The more he struggles, the worse things seem to become; for by fighting against life, he increases its disharmonies.

When, however, man is willing to be guided by an intelligence and wisdom that are infinite, all the Power of the Infinite is his, and *"all the Divine Forces hasten to minister to his eternal joy"*.

Man, however, quite naturally, is not willing to follow blindly that which he does not understand; therefore, this little work will endeavour to explain life and the laws and principles underlying it. Then, when the seeker after Truth understands life and its purpose, he will gladly cooperate with it, meeting it with joy and confidence, looking upon each day as a further opportunity to step up higher.

H.T.H.

Chapter Sixteen

Meeting Life in the Right Spirit

In a previous booklet, ***The Power to Overcome*** I tried to show how much depends upon our attitude towards life. If we look upon it as evil, it becomes, to *us*, something that is evil and very much to be dreaded and feared. If, however, we regard life as good, as something that is always trying to do us a good turn, we find that it *is* good. Therefore, simply our changed attitude towards life, is, in one sense, sufficient to transform it.

The great secret of successful living is to meet life in a spirit of co-operation, instead of antagonism. Until we realise that life is good and friendly, we oppose it at every turn; consequently, our troubles and disharmonies are increased and multiplied. Before, however, we can realise or even believe that life is good, we must know something about it. We must understand what its purpose and aim are, for then we shall not only know what to expect from it, but we shall also know how to deal with it, and in what attitude to meet it.

The object of life is twofold.

Firstly – to learn through experience, build up character, and attain wisdom.

Secondly – to take our share, small though it may appear to be, in the work of the universe, and in the unfolding of the divine plan. To love and serve others. To be instruments through which the divine life flows.

During the war[1] a general said to a friend of mine: *"if your officers were as happy under you as your men are, yours would be a perfect command"*. Quick as lightning my friend rapped out: *"They are not here to be happy and comfortable, sir, they are here to do their duty, to think of their men before themselves, and to set a good example to those below them"*. This reply describes very succinctly the underlying principle of life. The principal object of life is not to be merely happy and comfortable, but to gain experience and to learn wisdom. Until we understand this, we meet life in the wrong spirit, and thus increase our difficulties and multiply our troubles.

To one who looks upon his incarnation here merely as an opportunity for enjoyment, life must ever be a series of disappointments. Unless illumination comes to them, thinking people reach the stage, sooner or later, when they come to the conclusion that life is not worth living. They continue to live because they feel that it is their duty to do so, and because they refuse to play the coward's part, but life to them has lost its savour. They are so unhappy, they no longer wish to live.

---

1. The First World War, 1914-1918.

Life is an enigma to those who do not look upon it in the right light. There is no explanation to it, for it appears to be nothing but a purposeless, joyless round of daily existence. *"What,"* they exclaim, *"is the use of it all! I have lost the innocence and pure happiness of my childhood; I have tasted the fruits of sin and pleasure and found them bitter; while the things to which I looked forward so eagerly are either removed from my reach, or, now that I have obtained them, are utterly disappointing"*. Again, they may say: *"what is the use of this bitter farce that is called life? Those whom I loved dearer than life itself, and better far than my own soul, are taken from me. Life is nothing but a ghastly mockery; something that gives only to take away again"*.

It is obvious that if we expect life to give us merely happiness and a comfortable, vegetable-like existence, and instead it gives us disciplinary experience, which may be far from pleasant [but through which we can win happiness], we are bound to be disappointed. It is also obvious that so long as we look upon life not as a means of discipline, but as a "joyride", that we shall continue to make this mistake and consequently be disappointed.

If, however, we understand that this life is a visit to a training school, where we have the opportunity of learning valuable lessons, we are not disappointed; indeed, we are pleasantly surprised, for, if we meet life in the right spirit, endeavouring to profit by experience, we find that great happiness becomes ours, in spite of griefs, partings and changes.

When we realise that we are immortal, spiritual beings, passing through this life, inhabiting this body and experiencing our present restricted consciousness, largely for the sake of experience, the building up of character and the attaining to wisdom, how differently we regard life. Every experience passed through is something gained; every difficulty overcome is something added to our character; every grief experienced is for the mellowing and enriching of the soul. Whereas, formerly, every trouble, or so-called disaster, every grief, or apparent loss, was felt to be an injustice, now these things are seen to be a distinct gain. Hurrah! Here is another trouble to meet, another difficulty to overcome, is the spirit in which life's discipline is met by one who has gained the right viewpoint.

Life is a splendid privilege and a glorious adventure. No matter what we may have to meet in the way of discipline, we have the strength and the power to overcome. Also, and this is of great importance, if we meet every test or trial as it comes, and overcome it, never trying to shirk it or run away from it, or rebel against it, life can have no terrors for us. We become conquerors and find that life is good and gracious, instead of a terrible thing to be feared, or at best, to be endured with fortitude and resignation.

We come into the world naked, and we leave it in the same condition, except for the character we have built up, the wisdom we have learned and the love and service which we have given to our fellows. Character and wisdom, when gained, are eternal. They become part of the individual soul. No matter how painful our experiences in this life may be, the lessons learned, the character added, and the wisdom gained are worth far more than all the suffering entailed. Further, when once a lesson has been learned, the experience which taught the lesson never has to be repeated. That experience is done with, once and for all. If troubles keep repeating, it shows that our lesson has not been learnt.

When once we understand this, every experience of life is a source of satisfaction. When once we have learnt our lesson or built-up strength of character where once weakness existed, we have great cause for rejoicing, for we know that, not only have we become immeasurably richer, but we shall never have to pass through a similar experience again.

One of the greatest mistakes that we can make is to oppose change. The older in years people become, the less they like changes. They want the old order of things to remain. They tell us that *"the country is going to the dogs,"* and that the world is going to the devil. They forget that there must always be change in the external world, simply because it is in a state of becoming. It is its nature to change, but through this continual change God works out His perfect plan.

We may smile at the good people who expect the world to stand still, but most of us are no better ourselves, as far as our own individual life is concerned. It seems natural to oppose change, yet it is the very worst thing that we can do and is often the cause of great disharmony. When we oppose change, we go against the divine purpose of our existence; we drive away the blessings that are seeking us, and create a great upheaval in our life, involving much unnecessary suffering. This upheaval, painful though it be, is the Spirit's way of seeing that we do not rob ourselves altogether of the benefits of this life or escape its blessings. This is why people often say, speaking of a disaster (so-called) in their life, that it was a blessing in disguise. It was, because the spirit always works everything together for good; but, if they had learnt their lesson sooner, the upheaval in their life would have been unnecessary, and therefore it would never have occurred.

As a rule, upsets in the life are either the result of opposing change or are due to the leading of the spirit. Changes in the life should not be attributed to some evil influence, but to the leading of the spirit of truth, who is always endeavouring to bring us into wisdom and understanding. Therefore, the changes of life are always good and not evil and should be co-operated with instead of opposed. One who will do this will find the disharmonies of his life reduced enormously, for he will be working with the law instead of against it; he will be following out the divine purpose of his life.

Secondly, the object of life is also that we should take part in the work of the world and to help in the unfoldment of the divine plan. Many of us are not doing this. Some have incomes which they have to earn, therefore, they are satisfied and take no share in the labours of humankind. Others work because they have to, but they do not do it willingly or in the right spirit, therefore, they cut themselves off from the source of all joy and satisfaction.

One who is content to live on an independent income, living a self-centred life, receiving but never giving, cuts himself off, in consciousness, from the richer, fuller and more abundant life. He lives a restricted, starved and feeble life and every effort he makes to enter the fuller life of God, results in failure. It is the ambition of some people to possess an independent income, and to do nothing but live for themselves and their immediate family circle. They do not know the laws of life and being, otherwise they would not desire anything of the kind, for such a life is the most poverty-stricken life that it is possible to live.

If a person does not have to work for a living, it does not necessarily follow that they can take no part in the work of the world. Many people write to me and say they have never had to work for a living; therefore their life has been ruined and they have never known the zest and joy of living which busy workers experience, neither have they ever found happiness. Just because a person has means, however, need not keep him out of the kingdom of joyous souls who share the burden of the work of the world, for each can share in it, if he will. The disadvantage of having no need to work need not prevent those of independent incomes from sharing in the world's work. Voluntary work can always be found. There are many movements and organisations having for their object the uplift of mankind, which cannot afford to pay for labour, and which can be helped by voluntary assistance. But such voluntary work must be taken seriously. Just because it is voluntary, must be no excuse for such labour to be spasmodic, inefficient and unreliable. If work is to be of any value, it must be efficient and dependable. No half-hearted efforts are of the slightest use. Many organisations are sick of voluntary assistance, simply because some unpaid workers are inefficient and unreliable, looking upon themselves as superior, privileged people who can do as they please and who must not be spoken to or corrected. Such help as this is of but little use to any organisation. Voluntary work should be taken as seriously as paid work; it should be done at least as efficiently and thoroughly and should be engaged in as strenuously as the strength will allow.

The majority of those who have to work for a living, have to work almost to the limit of their strength. They have, literally, to bear the heat and burden of the day. Those who work voluntarily should also spend and be spent to the same extent. They must feel the burden of the world's work and share in it. Let them feel weary at the end of their day's toil, and they will find a satisfaction and peace of mind to which they have hitherto been strangers.

Further, life is an opportunity for service. The great underlying Law of Life and the Universe is Love. The law of service is, of course, part of the greater Law of Love. The Law of Love splits itself up, so to speak, into subsidiary or minor laws, but it embraces them all. Love embraces all: Love gives all: but the Law of Love demands of each one of us that we give all. It demands of each one of us that we become living embodiments of itself - giving all and embracing all in our love. If we do not do this, we are out of harmony with life: we are striking discordant notes on life's instrument, from which only love can produce the melody of true happiness, peace and joy.

The whole universe is held together by love - love in the form of inherent principle and love in action, i.e. service. Those who are strong help the weak, and those who are higher reach down and help the lower. Jesus taught us absolute truth, and if religious people had followed his teaching instead of doctrines and beliefs which are not only absent from his teaching but all quite foreign to it, the world would be quite a different place to what it is. Christ taught us that the way to the Kingdom is by loving God with all our heart, soul and mind, and fellow man as much as ourselves. Love to God, our spiritual source, and love to our fellow man - this is indeed the way of life, for it leads to unity and wholeness and oneness which is the great secret underlying diversity. Further, the great teacher taught us the greatest of all lessons in service when he washed his disciples' feet.

Many are prepared to serve the world as leaders but are not willing to undertake the humbler tasks of life. Many complain because they cannot serve in some great and glorious cause; every avenue of service is closed to them, so they say, and just as firmly believe. Yet it is not so. The way of service is open to all. Before we can be called to larger service, we must be faithful in the smaller, so-called, things of life. We can serve life and our fellows in a multitude of ways. We can serve by doing our daily tasks more perfectly than ever we have done them in the past. The fact that no one, as far as human wisdom can see, can ever benefit thereby, or because it is certain that we in any event cannot, in any way, benefit from our improved work and service, does not matter.

There is a spiritual debit and credit account kept, which not only rewards us as regards character, really our greatest wealth, but also rewards us in this life. The person who is careful not to do more work than he is paid for, shuts the door of success in his own face. The results, however, are more far-reaching than this, for one who does this cuts himself off from the Divine Life; he isolates himself, in consciousness, from the unity of the whole: he becomes a barren tree, yielding no fruit, and because of this, begins to disintegrate and perish. One, however, who serves far better than ever he can be paid for, comes into unity with the life of God, and the life of God in his fellow man, thus entering into unity with the whole. Such a life is always richly blessed, but often in ways unknown to outsiders. While another, less honest, may snatch a fortune by dubious means, and, while driving about in his lordly limousine, may splash with mud those who are his superior in every sense of the word, yet he can never be truly successful, and his life remains unblessed. One who can see behind external appearances sees a poor, miserable, starved, unhappy soul - an unfruitful tree that is drying up by the roots.

Not only can we serve in our daily tasks, by doing our work more efficiently than before - more expeditiously, more accurately and more perfectly - we can also serve better by following our employment from a different motive. Instead of working solely for the money we get, or the fame we win, we can look upon our work as a sacrament, and make it an offering of love to life and to the world. When we look upon our work as a holy thing - an offering to life [which is God, for God is the life] and to our fellows - we not only come into line with Christ's teaching, but we make it impossible for us ever to be slovenly or half-hearted or dishonest in our work. [All inefficient work is dishonest.] Our work becomes too holy and sacred a thing to be neglected, or to be delegated to others. Instead of being an irksome task, our work is seen to be a glorious opportunity to serve.

Neither does it matter really how humble or insignificant our work may appear to be. While not in itself insignificant or contemptible, it, if performed in the true spirit of service, may prove to be the gateway to greater things. But, even if it does not lead to greater things, in a material sense, there is always the spiritual debit and credit account being kept, which rewards us in true blessedness of life. Those who serve truly, in this way, earn those rare and precious possessions such as peace, happiness, joy, satisfaction, etc, which all the money in the world cannot buy. Happiness, peace, these are what all the world are seeking. What would millions of people give to possess them? Yet they can be had by those who will harmonise their lives with the laws of life and being.

Further, we can serve life and our fellows in other ways. There are always those around us who are below us in evolution and unfoldment who need help and succour. In helping these weaker ones, no reward, not even gratitude, must be looked for. We must learn to do things without hope of reward. We are rewarded indirectly for every kind action, and every effort made to help those who need help reacts upon us, but, as far as gratitude is concerned, the less we expect it the better, for unevolved souls are, as a rule, though not always, lacking in this quality. They expect to get everything for nothing, and do not realise what they must give in order to receive. What is done for them is very often taken as a matter of course, or even looked upon with disfavour. Of course, it is impossible to help people by making life easier for them. The only way by which we can help our less-evolved brothers and sisters, is by helping and encouraging them, not by attempting to make life easier for them, which only makes their difficulties loom larger than ever. By trying to make life easier for them, we actually make it more difficult. By encouraging them to overcome life's difficulties, we help them in the only possible way; for as they become stronger, life to them becomes correspondingly easier.

To help people in this way is, however, not easy. Many resent it and say: *"It is all very easy for you to talk, you don't have my difficulties"*. It is not easy to get them to understand and realise that they are stronger than their difficulties and can conquer them if they will only try. Again, we can serve and bless others in the small things of life. We can draw a bucket of water for an aged neighbour, or chop up her firewood, or feed her pig, or dig her garden, or perform any other kindly act that may be necessary. Those who live in towns and who are thus divorced from these simple duties, can perform other acts of kindness and neighbourliness.

We can also serve and bless others by our thoughts. We can refuse to think or speak evil of anyone. When scandal is broached, we can change the subject: when people's characters are vilified, we can speak kindly of them: when others are criticised and evil motives imputed to them, we can, instead, see only their good points and their finer qualities.

We can also hold others in thoughts of love and goodwill. We can, in time, develop into a sort of broadcasting station of love and goodwill thoughts. Our eyes become too pure to see evil, but they can penetrate beneath the exterior of our fellow men and see the good inherent. Indeed, one can even see the glow of the indwelling spiritual self, or at any rate, realise that *it*, the God within, is there.

Although it is departing, somewhat, from our subject, it may help readers to point out that our love and goodwill thoughts should not be directed only and solely to human beings but should be extended to all creation. It is only love that can restore and redeem creation and cause *"the wolf to dwell with the lamb, and the leopard to lie down with the kid"*. People sigh for the coming of Christ's Kingdom, but it is here now, for all who will enter it through the gateway of service and love. Jesus said, *"I am the door of the sheep"*, and it is by *doing* his sayings that we find the Kingdom of God. Therefore, let our love and sympathy be as wide and embracing as the love of God.

Let us unite ourselves with the whole family of God's creation in the fellowship of love. Let us see God in the dawn and the sunset; in the hush of calm and the tumult of storm; in the flowers at our feet and in majestic trees; in birds and in animals; in colours and scents; in sea and lake; in mountain and valley; in hill and plain. Let us find God in the spirit of the woods and the brooding spirit of the sea; we can even find God in the spirit of the hive and that of the ant-hill.

God is all in all; therefore, *He is the all in the all*. He is the one pervading life, and this life, in all the innumerable life of Nature, calls to the life of God in us. By coming into conscious unity and harmony with this greater, immanent, universal life of God in all things, our life becomes mysteriously altered and transformed. Indeed, our exterior world becomes changed also, for we are visited by times of illumination, when everything around us glows with the presence of God.

We can also help and serve others by our prayers. We can never look to God on behalf of another soul, without bringing blessing upon the one for whom we intercede. We do not know in what form the blessing will come, but we can be certain that good will manifest in the form that is best. It is impossible for us to tell what is best for another fellow creature. If we pray for a specific trouble to be removed, we may be doing that person a grave disservice, for to rob a life of its disciplinary experience is to do harm instead of good. Therefore, instead of interfering with another person's life, we realise on their behalf, the truth of being. By so doing, we raise up their consciousness nearer to a realisation of the truth, and thus make possible the manifestation of harmony and order in their life, in place of disharmony and disorder.

Finally, life gives us the opportunity of becoming centres of divine life. We can become channels through which life and wisdom flow to others. Before this is possible, we must, of course, make living contact with our divine source and find our true place in the divine order. By loving God and our fellow man and by spending ourselves in service; by seeking God, also, in the quiet of our souls, and by meditation, this contact can be made. The false walls of separateness become broken down, and we enter into oneness. We may not become spiritual healers in the strict sense of the word, but we become unconscious healers, for wherever we go we share a health-giving influence, a healing magnetism or virtue, which blesses those who come in contact with us.

Being in real, living, vital contact with the one, supreme, universal life, we enjoy an abundance of life, energy and power to serve and endure. As we feel within us the power of the Infinite Life, and realise our oneness with the One Inexhaustible Source, our life becomes transformed. We pass from feebleness to strength, from separateness and weakness to almost boundless power.

Chapter Seventeen

Life is Good

From what has already been said, it is obvious that life is good and not evil[1]. Although life is a discipline, yet it is a good discipline. As soon as we realise that life is not for mere passing pleasure, or even for mere comfort; as soon as we understand that the object of life is not that we should be amused, but that it is a glorious opportunity for character building, the learning of wisdom and of service to the whole, life becomes different. Hitherto life has had to prod us and

---

1. Life is good because it comes from God (Good). I am not now speaking of the breath of God within us, which makes life in this body possible, but all of our journey through this material world with all its experiences of joy and sorrow. We are propelled through life, not of our own will, but through a greater will. The will of the highest has projected us through our evolutionary journey up till now and will continue to do so through the ages. This will is not evil, neither is it foolish; it is the will of the Infinite Love and wisdom. Therefore, life, with its experiences, is both infinitely wise and infinitely loving.

make us go forward by all sorts of painful and unpleasant methods. If we will not become hard soldiers willingly, then we must learn to endure and build up character through adversity and suffering. When, however, we realise what a life is for, and go forward willingly and eagerly, it no longer has any need to prod us or to lash us with the whips of adversity.

After all that can be said, the great point is: how do we regard life? Do we look upon it as bad or do we regard it as good? If we regard it as bad, it is bad to *us*. Our life reflects our inward mental states. *"As a man thinketh in his heart, so is he"*, and it follows that as a man thinks so also is his life, for his life is a reflection of what a man is in character, attitude of mind, belief and thought. If we regard life as evil, it becomes filled with evil. If we look upon life as something to be feared and dreaded, then we find that it is full of experiences to be dreaded. On the other hand, if we look upon life as good, and affirm the truth, no matter how black appearances may be, we find that life *is* good; that no evil can come to us and that everything works together for good.

People on every hand are suffering from the pessimism of their thought. Pessimism brings suffering and unhappiness. It is opposed to the purpose of life, which is expression and expansion in ever increasing beauty and perfection. Pessimism is a savour of death unto death, but there is a divine optimism which is a savour of Life unto Life.

Life is good, and its tendency is ever upwards. The divine purpose is that we should live a richer, fuller and more spacious life. More perfect expression is the truth about life. No matter how high we may climb, there are infinite heights before us - greater beauty, greater love, greater service and greater revelations of divine wisdom. Because of this, pessimism is utterly opposed to truth. It is destructive to a degree. Instead of adding to life, it takes away, for it cuts us off, in consciousness, from the divine life and power.

Pessimism is death, and those who indulge in it live in the shadows and twilight. Yet they might get back in the sunshine of God's reality if they only would. The reality is joy and peace, happiness and health, abundance and well-being. The shadows of pessimism are depression and turmoil, misery and ill health, poverty and distress. They are not the reality, but only the shadows cast by a pessimistic misconception of the truth.

Some readers may say: *"How can I help being pessimistic, when life is such a dreary round and is so hard and so cruel?"* I might well answer by asking this question: *"How can your life be any different from what it is, if you continue to maintain your pessimistic outlook on life?"* The painful circumstances are simply the result of disharmony within. Life is good, flowing from the one central source of *life itself*, which is infinitely good - *good itself*. If then, this life manifests in painful or disharmonious form, it is because it has been transformed, so to speak, through a wrong attitude of mind and outlook, a wrong habit of thought, with the consequent clashing of will against Will. Thank God, we are all bound for a glorious destination, and even if we are out of harmony with life and its purpose, we shall ultimately "arrive", but our journey must of necessity be a painful one. Thanks be to the wisdom and love of God, we get there, but we make our journey a painful one if we do not get into harmony with life and its purpose.

The pessimism of which we have spoken is not only on the surface but may also be an obsession of the subconscious mind. Many people are unaware of what is called "subconscious cerebration". The subconscious mind is always thinking, and, if it thinks pessimistically, produces what we may call 'evil' in the external life, in the form of disease, ill health, failure, unhappiness or other disharmony. A person may be bright and cheerful, apparently, on the surface, yet pessimistic below the surface. The subconscious mind, however, can become changed, in course of time, by a process of thought transmutation. [2] Every thought that is pessimistic and opposed to the true purpose and tendency of life; every thought that denies that life is good and desirous of bringing yet greater good into expression, must be transmuted into thoughts which are in harmony with eternal truth.

---

2. ***Thought Transmutation,*** by Henry Thomas Hamblin.

Chapter Eighteen

A Revolution in Our Thought Life

Just as the thought of deity brings a universe into being, so also do our thoughts create, to a large extent, our external world and environment. Therefore, if our lives are to be harmonious, we must think with the law of being and the divine plan of the universe and of life. Let it be said here that we do not have to put the universe right, for the infinite mind makes no mistakes. The usual ideas of prayer are the begging and beseeching of God to repair some mistake He has made, or to redress some wrong He has committed. God's life is perfect, and we are sharers in this one life. We live our life with God. As God lives His life from day-to-day and from age to age, so do we share His life from day-to-day, from age to age, and it depends upon our attitude of mind and soul and habit of thought as to whether our life is full and abundant, harmonious and peaceful, or barren and poverty-stricken, discordant and full of turmoil.

We have not to alter the life of God, for this is perfect, as is our life also, but we do have to alter our attitude towards it. We have to adjust ourselves entirely to our new knowledge and conception of Life. We have to know the Truth, become established in this Truth, and then live in the consciousness of Truth.

We have to revolutionise our thought life. We have to think in harmony with truth and in terms of truth. We have to think from the standpoint that life is good in every possible way, and that the very worst it can bring us is a much needed and valuable discipline or experience.

To think from this standpoint necessitates an entire reversal of thought. Examine your thoughts and you will find that they centre around a fixed idea or belief in evil. This belief that life is evil is an obsession in the subconscious mind. This belief and this obsession must be eradicated. How can this be accomplished? There are two ways, which may be briefly described here. They are as follows:

1. Changing entirely their conscious thoughts, so as to transmute them from bad to good, from error to truth.

2. Making statements of absolute truth and repeating them at certain times. Statements of truth destroy error and help to awaken an inward understanding of truth. This is what sets us free.

If we are to think from the standpoint of truth, we must never criticise either our fellow creature or any experience of life. It is God's life, and God's universe, and God makes no mistakes - His ways are perfect. Criticism is destructive; it destroys and kills but never builds up. Examine yourself and watch yourself closely and see how prone you are to criticise the weather, other people, and certain experiences of life. You will find that you have been sitting in ceaseless judgement on your fellow creatures, and continually condemning God, who is the author of that which you criticise. *"Judge not that ye be not judged"*, said Jesus, *"for with what judgement ye judge, ye shall be judged: and with what measure ye meet, it shall be measured to you again"*. How easy it is to see the truth of this statement. By criticising and judging we cut ourselves off from the divine harmony and shut ourselves out from the perfect unity and peaceful operation of the whole. All our criticisms come back in the form of frictions, disharmonies, disasters and cares.

Make a pledge at this point never to criticise again. Declare now that you will never criticise your fellow creatures, for their life is the life of God and their development and unfoldment are in the hands and under the guidance of the spirit of truth. Declare also that you will never rail against life or look upon it as evil or cruel. Your life is the outcome of infinite wisdom and love, and every discipline is the highest possible manifestation of Good. Declare also that you will never criticise the weather. In the first place, there may be nothing wrong with it, in reality; and in the second place, whatever may be wrong with it is not due to divine wisdom and love having made a mistake, but to the discordant thoughts of humankind, the disharmonies of which affect nature.

Abstaining from criticism, however, although a tremendous step in the right direction, is, after all, only negative. It is like the goodness of some people, which consists merely in an absence of certain sins and vices. We must not merely abstain from criticism and railing against life, but we must think, speak, act and live in the knowledge that life is good and that all is well. This is living an affirmative, constructive life in harmony with God, instead of a destructive life opposed to the universal life and purpose.

Not only is it necessary that we become changed in thought, word and action, it is also imperative that the truth should be impressed upon that greater part of us which is below the level of consciousness.

This can be accomplished in two ways.

1. By spending a few minutes night and morning in quiet thought, withdrawing from the external life and making contact with the *great within*. Having put aside all thoughts of exterior things, repeat a definite statement of truth. Declare that life is good, that all is divine wisdom and love in manifestation. Deny the reality of evil and affirm the allness of good. Use your own words, not mine, but express this great central thought that life is good, *in every respect*; now there is only one power which also is good; that there is only one law, which is love; and one purpose, which is infinitely kind.

2. Whenever you meet difficulty, trouble, apparent disaster and other sense evidences of evil, which suggest to you an evil cosmic purpose, turn away from the external life of sensation, appearance and personality, and make contact with the great reality and principle. Then repeat your statement of truth and take your stand upon it, refuse to be moved from the position

you have taken up. Then watch truth manifest in your life instead of error. Turn to God and declare truth, and error must be swept away, until you see that there is nothing but good and nothing but love.

The only remedy for the ills of life is truth; the only way life can be transformed is by thinking, speaking and acting truth and living and serving in its light and power.

Afterword

LIFE AND POWER

Jesus said: *"The Kingdom of God is within you"*. That is the last place most of us would think of looking for it. We look everywhere, but within ourselves - in a distant heaven, in mortifications of the body; in difficult doctrines and theologies; in complicated religious systems; in wonderful revelations of wonderful seers; in forms and ceremonies; in philosophies; in metaphysics; in visions and ecstasies; in fact, in every place and in everything but the right one.

Finally, we look within and discover, as William Law tells us, that the Life, Power and Presence of God are within our own soul.

It comes as a shock to most of us when we discover that the Power is in us, and not in our circumstances.

In an instant of time, we become identified with the inward, real spiritual being who is born in us from above, and which never has been sick, never has sinned, and which can never die. *"The first man is of the earth, earthy. The second man is the Lord from Heaven"*. Or as other translators put it: the first man comes from the ground, but the second man from Heaven.

Which means, so I like to think, that we, as animals, are formed out of the elements of this planet, in the same way as all other animals, and have the same sort of life which has its day and then passes away. That is the first man, of the earth, earthy. But there is within us a man of quite a different quality, come down from Heaven, and belonging to Heaven.

Jesus said that except a man be born again of the Spirit from above, he cannot enter the Kingdom of Heaven. In other words, we have to discover our true selves. Our spiritual consciousness has to be opened and unfolded, so that we find the Kingdom of God within us; or, as William Law says, the Life, Power and Presence of God in the soul.

There is a spiritual innermost to everything. There is the real universe, of which this present time-space world which we cognize through the medium of this "vile" body, as St. Paul called it, is merely an imperfect reflection. There is a Perfection which is beyond perfection: a Wholeness which is beyond wholeness: an Order which is beyond order. All that we can see, or know, is but an imperfect reflection, or appearance, of the Hidden perfection which is invisible.

At first, we are conscious only of the external and material. But, when we become spiritually unfolded, we become conscious of the Real and Eternal.

As I said a moment ago, it comes as a shock to most of us when we realise that the Kingdom of God is within us – that the Life, Power and Presence of God are in our own soul, and that there is perfection behind or within everything. We can say: "Because the Life and Power and Presence of God are in our own soul, the trials and troubles of this present existence cannot affect us unduly".

We realise that our life, which outwardly may be disharmonious, has really an inner perfection which is entirely orderly, beautiful and harmonious. If the Kingdom of God is within me, then why all this exterior trouble and disorder, we may ask ourselves? We may think, because we have discovered the inner Kingdom of order, wholeness and perfection, that we should henceforward enjoy greatly improved health and circumstances.

This does not mean that we practise a form of magic. What it does mean is that as a result of finding the Kingdom of God and His righteousness, or Divine Order, all necessary things are added.

Jesus taught that we should put first things first: that we should not worry over, and be anxious about, the things of this life, but instead find the Inner Kingdom. As a result of doing this, so we are definitely promised, all necessary things will be added to us. Instead of our running after them, they come seeking us. Instead of being seekers after all the things necessary for a normal life, we become the sought.

Finding the Kingdom and practicing the Presence of God tend to bring our life back to a state of normality. The Divinely normal is a state of orderliness and completeness.

It is so easy for us, when we are beginners, to go wrong at this point. When we realise that the Power is in us and not in circumstances, we are in danger of going off at a tangent, in an attempt to smash the circumstances which have galled us for so long. But, through so doing, we may go against the real pattern of our life, thus creating disharmony, instead of finding the interior harmony, which is what we're all seeking and longing for, did we but know it.

Jesus taught us to seek first the Kingdom of God and His righteousness, after which all necessary things would be added to us. We should not try to smash circumstances by the misuse of spiritual power. Instead, Jesus tells us to find God and enter into union with Him; after which, our life will become adjusted according to an inner Divine pattern.

Those who have had to focus such things as magic lanterns, bioscopes, etc., know how all-important it is that the lens should be accurately focused. If it is out of focus, the image on the screen is blurred and most unsatisfactory. But directly we bring the lens into focus, the image on the screen becomes perfectly clear, sharply defined and altogether satisfactory. The screen image is now a true reproduction of the slide or film inside the lantern. Yet it is the same lantern, the same light, the same everything. The only thing that has happened has been an adjustment. We adjusted the focus of the lens, and then everything was made right.

In the same way, when we find the Kingdom of God within us, and surrender to the Will of the Whole, desiring only that

Infinite Love and Wisdom should guide every step we take, then a Divine adjustment is made in our life.

Also by Henry Thomas Hamblin

The Way of the Practical Mystic

The Little Book of Right Thinking

The Power of Thought

My Search for Truth

The Story of my Life

Within You is the Power

Life Without Strain

Divine Adjustment

The Open Door

Life of the Spirit

His Wisdom Guiding

The Hamblin Book of Daily Readings

God Our Centre and Source

God's Sustaining Grace

The Antidote for Worry

www.ingramcontent.com/pod-product-compliance
Lightning Source LLC
Chambersburg PA
CBHW060616080526
44585CB00013B/851